Review for
chin cent by
mid June

The Prophets
Pioneers to Christianity

The Prophets
Pioneers to Christianity

—————◆—————

WALTER G. WILLIAMS

ABINGDON PRESS

NEW YORK ⍟ NASHVILLE

THE PROPHETS—PIONEERS TO CHRISTIANITY

SET UP, PRINTED, AND BOUND BY THE
PARTHENON PRESS, AT NASHVILLE,
TENNESSEE, UNITED STATES OF AMERICA

TO HONOR

My Father and Mother

Preface

As a pastor and professor it has been my privilege to teach Bible courses for many years. During that time I have read and studied the prophets of the Old Testament many times. I have found numerous study and devotional books giving me help in understanding the messages of these men, summarizing their teachings, and giving the time and place of their delivery. Few books tell us just what the functions of the prophets were, how they were related to other religious leaders, what the prophets' special contribution to religious thought was, and why in the twentieth century we feel a special kinship with the thought and spirit of the prophet.

It is my purpose in this volume to consider especially these little understood phases of the prophet's life and work, and to present the results of my own research on these subjects during the last dozen or more years. Some of these studies have been presented before various professional societies, others to my colleagues in the ministry of the Church. Requests from students and fellow ministers have persuaded me to put these results into printed form so that they may be more readily available for careful study. They are presented, not as the final word of my own thinking or for others, but that these suggestions may stimulate further research and lead us all to greater understanding of prophetic inspiration and the prophetic word.

The religion of the prophets has brought challenge and inspiration to leaders and laymen alike in various periods of church history. For this reason alone studies in the prophets should be encouraged. If in addition clearer understanding may be gained of the work and religious convictions of the prophets, then we are doubly rewarded. It is my hope that a

7

study of prophetic religion by the method and outline suggested in this book will bring knowledge and insights as richly rewarding to the reader as they were to the writer.

During the last century, and particularly during the last two decades, much information has been made available to the biblical scholar through the discoveries of the archaeologist and historian. So much is now known about ancient customs of religious writing which was not known formerly that it would seem appropriate to begin with a consideration of our written sources of information. It would also seem to be essential that we should give careful consideration to the special groups in society who were charged with the responsibility of making written records. This involves also a consideration of the parallel problem of the professional relationship between the two groups in society who gave us the written records, priests and prophets. Part One deals with these problems.

Prophetic religion is far greater than the messages contained in the books attributed to the prophets. There were many things accepted by the prophets without question as part of their religion which they did not feel called upon to discuss, challenge, or reiterate. A full understanding of prophetic religion involves therefore not merely a recapitulation of their individual and collective messages but an understanding of the religious climate in which they lived. To obtain this, it is necessary to draw upon many other books in addition to those written by the prophets. Nearly all the Old Testament books have been utilized in those chapters dealing with major religious concepts in Part Two.

One of the major contributions of biblical scholarship during the last century was to recognize that many biblical books are the compilation of the writings of several authors, not one, and that the writings come from various periods in Hebrew history. It should be noted that the tendency, particularly on the part of German scholarship, to analyze the books into sources, and to be content with labels for the various sources, has led to a wholesome reaction. The answer lies, however, not in refusal to recognize sources but in organization of the sources into chronological sequence and in seeing the changes which came as men received the messages of the religious leaders.

It should be noted also that the current mood to seek unity

in the Scriptures is fraught with danger. One approach is to seek unity through theology. There is no theology in the Old Testament. There is religion—a vast difference. In Old Testament times men arrived at very definite convictions. There was little attempt at systematized bodies of belief. In the period of canonization, to be sure, more attention was given to the religious implications in the writings being considered for inclusion in the official collection of religious literature. But even here the major consideration was the concept of God and prerogatives of organized religion. Some attention was given to the nature of man, what constitutes salvation, what is sin, and so on. Attempts to see unity in the Old Testament through theology apart from a consideration of the historical development of religious concepts is doomed to failure. Unity imposed by editing for canonization is far from being unity of thought across the centuries. The two should not be confused.

The Old Testament is the product of Hebrew and Jewish religion. It must be studied as such. To look upon Old Testament writings as "pre-Christian literature" is misleading. The utterances and writings of prophets and other religious leaders brought inspiration and guidance to the people for whom they were first composed. To use these documents merely as keys to unlock the secrets of the future, either in the days of Jesus or in the twentieth century, is to underestimate the concern in the mind of the prophet for the people of his own day. It is also important to recognize that Jesus frequently brought changed meanings and new insights. Jesus' concept of Messiah was not that of his forebears or contemporaries. He brought new dimensions to the kingdom of God. Personal salvation taught by Jesus differed greatly from national salvation so long sought by some Jews. It is necessary for us therefore to see not only the long historical development of major religious ideas which have come over from Judaism to Christianity but also the sharp differences between Jewish and Christian interpretation.

As a reader proceeds with this study, especially when he comes in Part Three to the consideration of the prophets as persons, he will find that the work is largely based upon five of the Old Testament prophets. Why only five out of so many? Unfortunately most of the prophets gave us little or no biographical information, and it is impossible for us to reconstruct a picture of their lives except by drawing almost exclusively upon imagination. It is hoped that the biographical and ideological treatment of five men, whom we count as the most significant of all the prophets, will enable the reader to come to a real appreciation of all the prophets as vital, living personalities.

Further justification for our consideration of these individuals following general summaries of prophetic thinking is easily found in the fact that while these men made their contributions to the various concepts discussed, each in turn made a contribution to religion which was so specifically his that special discussion is demanded. Some overlapping of material is perhaps inevitable, but great care has been taken to avoid unnecessary duplication.

It is my great desire that as the reader becomes aware of what happened in the lives of the prophets as they became conscious of the presence of God within their lives, he also may seek the same rich fellowship with God. Men in every age need artists in religion, those who can envision the eternal, the significant, and the infinite, and etch these visions so graphically that lesser men might share the inspiration. Such were the prophets of Israel, and such must be the religious leader in the contemporary world.

Some acknowledgments must be made. It is a pleasure to make them. No book is written in a vacuum. Guidance and inspiration have come to me from many sources. Thoughts from many books have become so much a part of me that it is impossible except in the case of direct quotation to give credit where credit is really due. Many teachers have had a part in my religious growth, particularly such men as Dwight M. Beck, Leslie E. Fuller, Frederick C. Eiselen, Ernest W. Burch, Edwin E. Voigt, Albert T. Olmstead, John M. P. Smith, William A. Irwin, James Henry Breasted, and John A. Wilson. To them I am deeply indebted. My colleagues have been most encouraging and helpful; William H. Bernhardt and Harvey H. Potthoff, editors in turn of *The Iliff Review*, made space available for the first experimental publication of some of the material appearing in these pages; President Harold F. Carr has offered many suggestions in the various stages of the writing of the manuscript; Martin Rist has carefully checked the typescript and has made important corrections and sug-

PREFACE

gestions; Ernest Lemieux, my student assistant, and Norma
Hubka, a student at the University of Denver, have given
valuable secretarial assistance. To all of them I offer these words
of appreciation.

My youngest son, Ed, remarked during these final days of
writing, "There's a lot of work in making a book, isn't there,
Dad?" Much of the work is done by others than the author. My
family has borne the "burden and the heat of the long day" in
many ways. Amy, John, and George have participated in study
groups in which some of this material has been tested, and Eva
has given me splendid help in the preparation of the final typescript. Above all, I am deeply grateful for the inspiration, encouragement, and kindly counsel I have received from my wife,
Mary Esther. Without her love and understanding this book
would not have been possible. My thanks to all of them.

Walter G. Williams

Contents

PART THREE

Men Who Blazed the Trail

PART ONE

Records of the Journey

1

New Sources of Knowledge

◆

THE MATTOCK OF THE ARCHAEOLOGIST AND THE PEN OF THE historian have made us aware of our glorious heritage. The phrase "the living past" is more than the title of a book;[1] it is a statement of fact. Modern culture derives from and is a continuation of the ancient world. Our days are organized into weeks and are divided into hours and minutes because we have continued a practice begun by the ancient Babylonians. Many of the words we use today, such as "star," "camel," "Easter," and "paper," are borrowed from the Babylonians and Egyptians. Much of our mathematical knowledge began in the ancient world. On a tablet from four thousand years ago is a mathematical problem the solution of which is dependent upon a knowledge of what was later called the "Pythagorean Theorem." Writing was first known to the world in those lands we have designated "Bible lands." Beginning first with rudely scratched pictures upon pieces of clay, man quickly learned to indicate his thoughts by using crude and later stylized pictures to convey his thoughts. This complicated method of writing was ultimately displaced by the invention of an alphabet. It too was discovered in the ancient Near East, and the very forms of some of our letters are directly traceable to the original shapes in which the Semites drew them. We are thrilled as we step into the starlight night; and gazing into the heavens, we are able to trace the outlines of the various constellations.

---

[1] Cyrus H. Gordon, *The Living Past* (New York: John Day Co., Inc., 1941).

15

We forget that these groupings of stars were recognized many centuries ago and that they still are known by the names given to them in an ancient day.

We are proud of our gains in medical knowledge, yet we should be immeasurably poorer had it not been for the skillful investigations of the ancient Egyptians. These ancients knew of the pumping action of the heart. They discovered that arteries carried the blood throughout the human system, but they failed to discover the circulatory system. The Hammurabi Code of four thousand years ago indicates that delicate surgical operations were performed in the land of Babylonia. Clay tablets found by the archaeologist tell of great dramas enacted in the temples. In detail are given the instruction for the seasonal portrayal of the continuing struggle between the forces of nature. Drama, though modified and adapted to the stage by the Greeks, began not with the Greeks but with the Semites.

The "zero," of prime importance in mathematics, was used early by the Assyrians. Babylonians divided the circle into 360 degrees. But these people had their limitations. Their problems were always practical problems and often solved by rule of thumb. For example, they did not know "pi" and regularly used the value 3 in finding the areas of circles, and so on. But they knew from experience that this was not correct; and they worked out correction tables so that if the diameter of the circle exceeded a certain length, they knew that a corresponding correction needed to be made in their estimate of the area of the circle.

The Egyptians were the first people of whom we have record to evolve a calendar based upon the movements of the sun. It is probable that weaving and the cultivation of grain began in the valley of the Nile, and it was there that glazing and the manufacture of glass were discovered. Cosmetics were first found in the oldest Egyptian burials. A study of the evolution of beads can be an interesting pursuit and is possible in any museum of Egyptian artifacts. Bead making was a fine art very early among the Egyptians, and the arrangement of some of the necklaces indicates extremely good taste. In the practical fields and in the fine arts we owe much to the inhabitants of the Near East, but it is only belatedly that we are recognizing

16

that debt. Let us examine more fully therefore the wealth of information now made available through the painstaking work of the archaeologist.

During the war years there was little excavation in the Near East, but this afforded opportunity to evaluate the materials already at hand. A number of significant texts have already appeared in which such evaluation is made,[2] others will undoubtedly be forthcoming. The rapid expansion of knowledge through this field of investigation, the spectacular discoveries made, and the extravagant claims made in some quarters all suggest the need for an appraisal of the values in archaeology for biblical studies. If we understand the purposes and methodology of the archaeologist, we may be enabled to read correctly the enlarging volumes of history. As we see the significance of interlocking cultural patterns, we shall be the better able to weigh the significance of Hebrew religious culture. As we trace the heritage of the past, we may understand something of its influence in the present; and the present may be liberated from the dead hand of the past as understanding comes to us.

Until the turn of the twentieth century there was little purpose in archaeology except to acquire treasures from the past for display pieces in our museums, and occasionally there were attempts to prove or disprove certain portions of the Bible. Science now recognizes that any investigator who seeks to prove or disprove any theory (as distinguished from testing) is likely to be biased in judgment and therefore unscientific. The only purpose of the modern excavator is to recover artifacts with such scientific skill and care that he can place in the hands of the historian materials from which ancient history may correctly be written. Such history may support Bible tradition, it may modify it or even contradict it, but that is incidental for the modern historian. Actually there are few specific dates in our Bible; and in the past we have been forced to string our

[2] C. C. McCown, *The Ladder of Progress in Palestine* (New York: Harper & Bros., 1943) ; Millar Burrows, *What Mean These Stones?* (New Haven, Conn.: American Schools of Oriental Research, 1941) ; Nelson Glueck, *The Other Side of the Jordan* (New Haven, Conn.: American Schools of Oriental Research, 1940) ; William F. Albright, *Archaeology of Palestine and the Bible* (3rd ed.; Westwood, N. J.: Fleming H. Revell Co., 1935) ; Albright, *Archaeology and the Religion of Israel* (Baltimore: Johns Hopkins Press, 1942) ; Jack Finegan, *Light from the Ancient Past* (Princeton, N.J.: Princeton University Press, 1946).

history of the Hebrew people, and particularly of their neighbors, upon insecure dates. Now we may approach the problem of their history with the confidence that the dates proposed by the historian have been carefully checked.

Similarly, obscure phrases in prophetic teaching are now alive with meaning because the same or similar phrases have been found in other literature and in new contexts. For example, it was thought strange that there should be a humanitarian provision in the Primitive Code of Exod. 34 prohibiting boiling a kid in its mother's milk. From a magical incantation text recovered from Ras Shamra we have the description of an ancient ceremonial designed to bring rain. The heart of the ritual was to boil a newly born kid in its mother's milk. It would seem probable therefore that the Hebrew regulation was not humanitarian but simply one of protest against a neighbor's religious practices.[3] Such insights are possible only after the archaeologist and historian have done their work, that of making available unbiased information from the past.

The methods used by archaeologists may be grouped under four heads. The first method was simply that of "pot hunting." Since practically all archaeological investigation is made possible by the generosity of benefactors, it is natural that such benefactors should expect results and recognition. Both demands were formerly answered by bringing back pretty pots for museum display, each display bearing tributes of praise to the generosity of the benefactor. Little scientific information resulted from this except as inscriptions were recovered accidentally.

The next method was in the direction of the scientific. It was discovered that in the ancient East many mounds were the result of one civilization piling on top of another. There were two major causes of this. First, buildings were usually constructed of mud brick or clay, and built on the surface of the ground. Disintegration came quickly, and the house owner simply leveled off the debris and built again on top of the old materials. In general, however, the level of an occupied site changed little during the occupation. But there were periods when the site was not occupied. The inhabitants may have been driven off by enemies. Fire may have destroyed the entire city.

[3] Cf. p. 81.

There were other causes. Second, an unoccupied city soon fell into decay to be covered quickly by sands from the desert. Those who reoccupied the site leveled off the ground and began their own construction without regard to what lay beneath. Only in the case of larger stone buildings were foundations sunk. If the earlier occupation was terminated by fire due either to accident or to enemy action, a layer of ashes can be distinguished between it and the succeeding level of occupation. The second method of excavation therefore proceeded from this knowledge. A pit was sunk through the mound, levels were carefully noted and measurements taken, and objects were photographed *in situ* before removal. This method is still used of necessity in some expeditions, but the chief objection is that the pit may give an inadequate sampling of the mound.

To correct this fault, a third method was used, that of cutting a trench across the entire mound and sinking it to virgin soil. A fourth method was simply a development of the third, to excavate the entire area by levels; and this is the method used whenever possible in any modern excavation.[4] The last three methods are all variations of stratigraphical digging and differ only in the extent to which the work is complete. Three cardinal principles must be obeyed meticulously: excavation by levels, careful and exact recording, and interpretation after comparison with other expeditions. The first two are field work; the last is frequently deferred until the return to the home base. The archaeologist must ever remind himself that the mound before him is a record of man's past and as he proceeds with the work of stripping the mound, that record is being destroyed. Unless he correctly records his evidence down to the slightest detail, that part of man's record will be lost. Careful recording is a primary requisite. A man may incorrectly interpret the evidence; but if he has honestly and painstakingly recorded the facts, the interpretation will be corrected later. If the evidence is incomplete or destroyed, correction is difficult.

Spectacular discoveries have naturally attracted attention, but they were not always the most important. The opening of King Tutankhamen's tomb occupied public attention for months, yet little new information was gained, for historians had already

[4] See Burrows, *op. cit.*, pp. 12 ff., for more detailed description of methodology.

carefully pieced together that portion of Egypt's history from other evidence. Egypt's great monuments have been known for centuries, but it was not until the discovery of the Rosetta Stone that men had found the important key to unlock Egypt's written treasures. Even after possession of the Rosetta Stone had been gained, it took years of work before scholars could actually read Egyptian hieroglyphs. In a similar way the key to the cuneiform writings was found in the Behistun inscription. Now after many years of work Sumerian, Babylonian, Assyrian, and Persian may be read with relative ease. New languages are being discovered from time to time, and we now have much information about nations we never knew existed. The story of man's growth is a fascinating one, and bit by bit that story is being pieced together. The volumes of ancient history are being enlarged constantly. Limitation of space permits only a brief glance at some of these volumes.

Until a few years ago little or nothing was known of the Sumerians, a non-Semitic people who occupied the Mesopotamian valley for centuries before the Babylonians came upon the scene of history. One of the oldest stories of creation is to be found in their literature. The Sumerians apparently came into the valley from mountainous regions and continued to worship the mountain deities. To accommodate their gods, they built artificial mountains on the tops of which the gods were presumed to reside. The Babylonians in turn built similar structures known as "ziggurats" for their gods. It is possible that the tradition of the Tower of Babel (Gen. 11:1-9) reflects this same pattern of thought. The Sumerians bequeathed their language to the priests of Babylon; and for centuries Sumerian was the religious language of Babylon, just as Latin is in use today in Roman Catholicism. Many "dictionaries" have been found in the Babylonian and other temples, giving the Babylonian meaning of Sumerian terms.

Fairly complete histories have been written of the Babylonians and Assyrians.[5] Among their literature are to be found the Tablets of Creation, the Babylonian and Assyrian Psalms,

[5] Cf. A. T. E. Olmstead, *History of Assyria* (New York: Chas. Scribner's Sons, 1923) ; and A. Goetze, *Hethiter, Churriter, und Assyrer* (Cambridge, Mass.: Harvard University Press, 1936).

temple records, and the records of the great military campaigns. One of the outstanding contributions was the recovery of the Hammurabi Code from the twentieth century B.C., and its parallels to the Covenant Code (Exod. 21-23) are of great interest.[6] It now appears that the Old Sumerian Code was borrowed and modified by the Babylonians, becoming the Hammurabi Code. In turn the law of the Babylonians was borrowed by the Canaanites and may have existed as a codified civil law about 1200 B.C. Then the Hebrews adopted it and made adjustments in the light of changing social patterns and religious concepts. The Covenant Code achieved its present form between 500 and 400 B.C.

The campaigns of the Assyrian leaders Tiglath-pileser III, Sargon, and Sennacherib are now well known through tablets, prisms, and monuments. The fuller knowledge of Assyria's strengths and weaknesses enables us to understand more fully the rise and fall of Hebrew political fortunes. It is interesting to note that even in that day military leaders always claimed victory, with negligible losses of their own armies and stupendous losses inflicted upon the enemy, even though a study of the map reveals that they had lost territory. Apparently these were strategic withdrawals.

To the northwest of Palestine in Asia Minor excavations have given us knowledge of the Hittites, Hyksos, and Hurrians, nations that were hitherto only vaguely known, with some historians denying their existence. The great political disturbances from Mesopotamia to Egypt are becoming increasingly clearer as more knowledge is gained of Asia Minor and the surrounding peoples. The Hittites moved in shortly after the beginning of the second millennium B.C. They contested, and successfully, the power that Egypt had over the northeastern Mediterranean and its adjacent lands. Hurrians meantime had pushed into northern Mesopotamia and became the ruling class. By the middle of the seventeenth century their influence was felt as far south as Egypt. The movements of Hittites and Hyksos, who conquered and controlled Egypt for many years, were be-

---

[6] An excellent translation of the Hammurabi Code is available in J. M. P. Smith, *Origin and History of Hebrew Law* (University of Chicago Press, 1931), pp. 181-222.

tween the Middle Kingdom and the New Empire. It is to this period that the Joseph stories undoubtedly belong.

Excavations in Palestine indicate that there was no time during Hebrew history when the influence of Egypt was not felt. Our knowledge of Hebrew history, therefore, has been greatly increased by the amount of information that has come to us from excavations in Egypt.[7] Among the contributions made by Egyptians to Hebrew culture are strong literary and religious influences.[8] It has been suggested that Hebrew monotheism roots back in the great religious reform of Ikhnaton; but it is certain that in the period when Egypt's influence could be presumed to be the strongest, at the time of Moses, the Hebrews were henotheists. Literary parallels have been noted between "The Hymn to Aton" and Ps. 104, "The Two Brothers' Tale" and the Joseph incident with Potiphar's wife, and "Sayings of an Egyptian Sage" and Proverbs.

Another group of documents recovered from Egypt are the famous Tell el-Amarna tablets, which were written in Palestine in the fourteenth century B.C. They are written in Akkadian (cuneiform), which was the international language of that day, and were sent to the Egyptian Pharaoh. The great turmoil in Palestine due to the infiltration of the Habiru, or SA.GAZ, is the subject of these tablets. These reports of Egyptian representatives, together with the evidence from Jericho which establishes a fall of that city about 1400 B.C., have been accepted as proof of the invasion of Palestine by the Hebrews in the fourteenth century. Meantime historical and biblical criticism had established a date of 1200 B.C. Further evidence has now been adduced which indicates that the conquest of Palestine by the Hebrews lasted for a long period and that in all probability there was more than one wave of migration into that country.[9] More evidence is needed, but it becomes increasingly clear that the Hebrews were not one people except for a short period under David and Solomon. Even then the ties were political and not of a common ancestry and culture.

[7] See J. H. Breasted, *History of Egypt* (1912); and G. Steindorff and K. C. Seele, *When Egypt Ruled the East* (Chicago: University of Chicago Press, 1942).

[8] Cf. Breasted, *Dawn of Conscience* (New York: Chas. Scribner's Sons, 1934).

[9] An excellent summary of biblical and archaeological evidence is given in H. H. Rowley, *From Joseph to Joshua* (New York: Oxford University Press, 1950).

One of the most startling excavations in recent years has been that at Ras Shamra on the north Syrian coast. The history of the town covers many hundreds of years, but our particular interest is in the alphabetic cuneiform tablets recovered from the close of the fifteenth and the beginning of the fourteenth centuries B.C. One tablet indeed lists the alphabet in virtually the order known to us through Hebrew and Phoenician writings.[10] Close parallels with Hebrew literature are being discovered constantly.[11] The literary parallels are more often found between Ras Shamra and the late priestly documents of the Hebrews than with the earlier Judean and Elohistic documents. Other parallels have been noted in the Hebrew Psalms, in Job, and in the book of Daniel. One of the heroes at Ras Shamra is named Dan (i) el. Claims have been made through the public press that the original Adam and Eve account and a reference to Abraham are to be found in these documents, but careful examination of photographs of the tablets reveals no such items. An analysis of the content of this newly discovered literature and the structure of the language will occupy us for many years, but the net result will be a better understanding of the Hebrews and their neighbors in that period of Hebrew entry into Palestine in its earliest stages.

Excavations within the borders of Palestine have helped us to fill in the details of Hebrew history which have often been omitted by writers of the Bible accounts. A picture of interlocking cultural patterns emerges. The land of Palestine was not an isolated region but was the link between the great civilizations in three continents: Asia, Africa, and Europe (by way of Asia Minor). Armies and caravans constantly traveled its roads, and cultural influences were many and varied. The Abraham stories fit that early period before the fertility religion had impinged upon Phoenician and Canaanite culture. There is no reference to the Baal cultus or fertility rites in the Abraham stories. The Jacob and Esau stories reflect the later pattern of the late eighteenth and seventeenth centuries. Still later the Joshua stories may be fitted into our knowledge

[10] I examined this tablet in the museum at Damascus, Syria.

[11] C. H. Gordon, *The Loves and Wars of Baal and Anat* (Princeton, N.J.: Princeton University Press, 1943) ; and C. F. A. Schaeffer, *The Cuneiform Texts of Ras Shamra-Ugarit* (New York: Oxford University Press, 1939).

of Egyptian history in that period when the Hyksos were in control. The invasions in the fourteenth to twelfth centuries are well attested by changes in pottery, the newcomers bringing much inferior types.

Evidence from figurines and temple areas indicates that by the last quarter of the second millennium B.C. the Baal religion had strong hold upon Canaan. Our Bible states that the father of Gideon, the Yahweh champion, was a follower of Baalism. The period of the Judges was one of confusion and clash. The great clash between Baalism and Yahwism, however, did not come until the time of the great prophets in the ninth, eighth, and seventh centuries. The luxury of the ruling classes in Samaria is well attested by the excavations in that area by Harvard University. Meantime the monarchy had come into being; and the declining power of Assyria and Egypt is clearly indicated in archaeological evidence, their decline making possible the rise of a new nation, the Hebrews.

The Hebrew nation was never strong except under David, for early in the reign of Solomon control of the colonies began to slip away. This placed the monarchy in an embarrassing position. Solomon solved this by raising funds by two methods, each attested by excavation. Solomon traded horses, and there were a number of centers at which stables were built for caring for horses in transit from the North to Egypt by way of Solomon, the middleman. Megiddo (Armageddon) is a notable example. Then Solomon entered the metal industry, and excavations at Ezion-geber, at the head of the Red Sea, indicate that considerable copper smelting was done there in Solomon's time. We know, too, that it was from this port that the fleet of Solomon, the only ships in Hebrew history, set sail.

And what of the contribution of the Hebrew? Excavations indicate that usually his material culture was decidedly lower than that of his neighbors. But he judiciously borrowed from those neighbors and benefited from them. It is in the field of religion, however, that the Hebrew made his greatest contribution. Oftentimes he needed to borrow literary patterns from his neighbors by which to express the religious discoveries he had made. A sixth-century priest took a polytheistic poem of creation and rewrote it in the light of his own belief, and has taught the world "in the beginning [one] God created." The prophets of the eighth century, however, were the first to assert a belief in one God.

It was in that same period that Amos gave us the teaching that creation is moral because the creator is moral. It was in that same half century, too, that Hosea insisted that this moral God had a love and concern for man. Down to this time the Hebrew had believed that religion was a matter of the covenant relation between the group as a group and the Deity. Jeremiah then Ezekiel asserted in the seventh and sixth centuries that religion was a matter of individual conduct. Then came the decline. Judaism descended to legalism and sacerdotalism, but there were enough brave pioneers who deviated from the accepted pattern that people were challenged. Their messages have been gathered into our Bible. Many of these heroes are nameless, but their messages still challenge.

Such people are worth knowing, and we are constantly seeking fuller information concerning the cultures that produced these leaders and their challenging messages. Some of that information will come from future archaeological expeditions; but enough historical information is now available to us to make new appraisals of the great religious pilgrimage of the Hebrew people, of those who were the outstanding leaders, and of some of the religious discoveries that have been so meaningful in our Christian heritage.

2

The Biblical Record Becomes Clearer

———————◆———————

THE MAIN SOURCE OF OUR INFORMATION CONCERNING THE growth of Hebrew-Christian religion is the Bible. Information that is made available through the work of the archaeologist and the historian provides the setting in which we may understand biblical stories. The reconstructed histories of the neighboring nations to the Hebrews give us an understanding of the political, social, and economic conditions in the periods during which various portions of our Bible were written. Nevertheless, it is to the Bible that we must turn to see the development of various concepts. As we compare these religious beliefs with the religious documents of neighboring people, some very interesting parallels and divergences are discovered. There is little doubt in the minds of most scholars today that there was free interchange of literature and sometimes of religious concepts between the Hebrews and their neighbors. Babylonian, Assyrian, Egyptian, Persian, Phoenician, and Greek each made his contribution to developing Hebrew thought.

Sometimes literary borrowings were direct with only little change in the material. At other times the document borrowed was greatly modified. It is quite likely that literature was borrowed from the Hebrew, though not as much attention has been devoted to this particular phase of cultural interdependence. Perhaps the most outstanding cases of such borrowing are first, the acceptance by the Christians of the entire Hebrew scripture; and second, the complete dependence of the Mohammedan Bible, the Koran, upon Hebrew and Christian scriptures. It seems logical then to assume that with such ready interchange of culture and concepts, and if we are to have an adequate understanding of any one segment of that general milieu, then we ought to have as full information as possible concerning the total environment. Yet it still remains apparent that our primary source of information concerning Hebrew-Christian religious development is the Bible. Whatever else we may say of the Bible, it is essentially a collection of man's religious experiences; and those experiences are gathered from many different periods of history. Failure to understand this has led to many misinterpretations of biblical statements.

In many ways our Bible is similar to an ancient mound. As the archaeologist approaches the mound, he presumes that it contains evidence of man's former residence in that area; but in addition he may learn from it how early man furnished his home, how he earned his living, what kind of food was obtainable, what his religious beliefs were, and what he thought about many aspects of life. If the archaeologist proceeds scientifically with his task of excavation, not only will he be able to give us early man's answers to these questions; but if the ancient site was occupied by man for many centuries, then it is possible for him to arrange his evidence so that we may see how man progressed in his thoughts and practices in each of the periods of occupation. Just so with our Bible: if it is possible for us to arrange our material in the chronological order in which it was written, then we ought to be able to see the growth of man's understanding of God, of his fellow man, of the world in which he lived, and to see also the changes in his religious practices.

It has long been recognized that there were constant changes in religious practice as the people responded to the biddings of religious leaders, but it has not been as clearly recognized that there were corresponding changes in man's religious concepts. One of the less fortunate aspects of the Protestant Reformation was that when challenged concerning their new practices, the reformers turned to the Bible for authority. This led inevitably to the same difficulty that the Roman Church faced, the need for a dependable authority; and just as the Church of Rome developed the dogma of the infallibility of the pope, so the Protestants arrived at the dogma of the infallibility of the Word, otherwise known as verbal inspiration.

Any authoritarian movement of necessity must have an absolute authority. In so far as Protestant groups have become authoritarian, just so far have they missed the genius of the great Reformation; and for the particular purposes of our present study they have missed the greatest values to be discovered in the Bible. The men to whom we turn today for our religious "authority" were individuals who dared to think for themselves, who refused to be bound by external authority, and who discovered in their own religious experiences principles and insights that were completely at variance with the accepted dogmas of their own day. That is why we read them today. They discovered, as we must discover for ourselves, that religion can never be dictated, it must be experienced.

In order that we may have the finest appreciation and the fullest understanding of the messages of the Bible, it has been necessary for scholars to devote themselves to four areas of study. A lack of understanding by the layman of the purposes of the scholar's work has sometimes led to misunderstanding and ofttimes to bitter denunciation. The scholar has often been responsible for much of the misunderstanding by writing only for other scholars or in a terminology that is not familiar to the layman. Unfortunate selection of terminology, for example, the word "criticism," has led to further tension in the field. Yet the fact remains that the essential motivation of the Bible scholar has been that all men might have the finest and most dependable information concerning the Bible. The four areas of investigation have all contributed to this one great purpose.

The first area is that of answering the question, "Is this particular part of the Bible preserved in the form in which it was originally written?" Whatever may be our particular theory concerning the origin of the biblical record, it has nevertheless been subject to human frailties since its original writing. Our oldest manuscripts are many centuries removed from the original writings.[1] During those centuries the Bible was copied by hand, sometimes by individuals who were not particularly thrilled with their task. Illustration of this fact is seen in a Latin Bible which had been copied during the Middle Ages by a monk. This monk had copied one biblical passage but apparently believed that he did not have time to begin another.

[1] The latest manuscripts to be found include a copy of the book of Isaiah dating perhaps as early as the second century B.C. In 1952 other ancient manuscripts were recovered including many Old Testament books, and material is still coming to light. Cf. Millar Burrows, *The Dead Sea Scrolls* (New York: Viking Press, 1955).

He passed away the time by making some scribblings in the margins, after which he wrote at the bottom of the page, "I wonder when the dinner bell will ring." When the copying of the Bible was done by such men, it is needful to ask, "Is this the message as it was originally written?"

At least two other human weaknesses impair the probability of our receiving the Bible messages in their original purity. In order to make the process of copying as inexpensive as possible, a system was worked out whereby one individual would read aloud from the original, and a number of writers would make their copies as he read. Under such circumstances the possibility of mistakes increased, for similar sounding words may be confused, punctuation be misplaced, and unfamiliar words misspelled or so badly bungled that the original is almost impossible to recover. The weakness of the human ear is matched by the weakness of the eye. Many copies were made by scribes who sought to copy carefully from an older document. But too often words and sometimes whole phrases were omitted or even duplicated because the eyes of the scribe were tired or otherwise defective. Occasionally an omitted sentence was recovered in proofreading and inserted in the margin or other available space. Still later copyists, working with the corrected copy, inserted the omitted sentence at the wrong place thus leading to a confusion of the message. It is to an attempt to correct such mistakes that many scholars have devoted themselves. The process is known professionally as "textual criticism" or sometimes "lower criticism." The terms are unfortunate but mean simply that we are attempting to get a copy as nearly like the original as is humanly and scientifically possible.

The second area of biblical scholarship is that of relating the various passages to the circumstances under which they were written. One of the difficulties we face in our attempts to understand the significance of the words of the prophets is that ordinarily only the message is recorded and not the circumstances or the time at which it was delivered. If we add to this the fact that most of the Bible books have only the titles that were given to them at a time much later than that of their writing, our difficulties are further increased. As a matter of fact the Jews today know many of these same books by different titles, usually derived from the opening word or phrases of the biblical book. The ancient documents had no titles.

The titles given at a later date too often added to confusion. For example, the books of Samuel, originally one book, bear the name of Samuel only because he is the great controlling figure in their history, not because he is the author of the books. Similarly, the Books of Law have long been known as the Books of Moses, not because Moses is the author, but because they contain the story of Moses and the giving of the law usually attributed to Moses. Later generations, unaware of literary history, have insisted that Moses wrote these books in spite of the fact that no claim is made within the books that Moses is the author. He is credited only with certain portions of the books. It has been discovered, also, that some books are compilations from other written sources no longer in existence. In our so-called historical books, Joshua to Chronicles, we have specific recognition of ten different sources with an eleventh source mentioned in the book of Numbers. These include the Books of the Wars of Yahweh; the Book of the Upright; chronicles of the northern and southern kingdoms; histories by the prophets Samuel, Nathan, and Gad; and two commentaries (see Num. 21:14; Josh. 10:13; II Sam. 1:18; I Kings 11:41; II Chr. 20:34; I Kings 14:29; I Chr. 29:29; II Chr. 13:22; II Chr. 24:27).

There are many clues by which the scholar is able to determine the period in which a book was written. The language structure, the vocabulary used, the specific references within the text to current political events, the stage of religious development reflected in the message of the book, and loan words and concepts from surrounding cultures are all clues by which we are able to discover the date and locality of a book or the portion of a book. How much more significant the book of Ruth becomes as we recognize that it was written not in the period of the Judges but in the late history of the Jews, and written not merely to portray a beautiful love story but as a protest against the narrow nationalism of the Jews in the late Persian period. The Jews were barring foreign marriages, divorcing foreign wives, insisting that they were a biologically pure people. The writer of Ruth not only tells a beautiful story but says in addition: How foolish to denounce foreigners when one of the ancestors of David, our greatest national figure, was herself a foreigner.

The fortieth chapter of Isaiah leaps into new significance as we discover that it was written at the close of the bitter Babylonian exile and that it echoes the new hope of deliverance that sprang up with the conquests of Cyrus the Persian.

> "Comfort, O comfort my people," says your God;
> "Speak to the heart of Jerusalem, and call to her,
> That her time of service is ended."
>
> (Vss. 1-2.)

These are words of hope and encouragement that have meaning only to a nation which has suffered. If we can recover the circumstances under which a book was written, we shall have gone far toward discovering the purpose of the writer; and only as we discover his purpose, shall we fully understand the writer's message. Seeking to relate a document to the purposes that inspired it is known as "historical criticism" and somewhat erroneously as "higher criticism." I prefer the phrase "historical evaluation." Misuse and misinterpretation of the results of this second area of investigation have denied to many people the information that was essential to their complete understanding of the Bible messages.

The third area of investigation is more easily understood. Our Bible was written in foreign languages and in cultures that were completely different from our own. If we are to have any understanding of the words of Jesus, they must be changed from the Aramaic in which he spoke, or from the Greek in which his words are first known to have been written, into the language which we use today. Unfortunately there are those who believe that the only language in which the Bible may appropriately be rendered is the Elizabethan English of the Authorized (King James) Version. Yet these same people are quick to assert that the Roman Church should read the Scriptures (or any other part of the service) in language that its worshipers understand. They forget that Latin has been a "holy language" far longer than seventeenth-century English. Furthermore, so long as we keep our religious literature in a language that is quite different from everyday life, just so long will religion be in danger of being an appendage to life rather than a vital part of it.

The work of translating would appear to be relatively easy, yet a moment's reflection will indicate how difficult that task can become. To translate from one modern language to another presents its difficulties. It is one thing to find equivalent words, but quite another to carry across ideas, particularly if an idiomatic expression is involved. Some expressions in one language are almost impossible of translation into another. I lived as a boy in England and came to America in my teens. I discovered to my horror that expressions which were perfectly acceptable in my native land had far different connotations in the land of my adoption. Bible writers used idiomatic Hebrew, Aramaic, or Greek, which varied from generation to generation. Add to this the fact that the meanings of some ancient words have long been forgotten, and the problem is made still more difficult. The so-called "musical phrases" in the titles of the Psalms are a case in point (e.g., 8, 9, 16, 22, and so on). The best that can be done for the time being is to transform the Hebrew letters into English letters and believe that the word is the name of a hymn tune, a pious hope at best. We ought to confess that these are untranslated Hebrew words even if we have printed them in English letters.

Some passages of our Bible are completely unintelligible in the original language. Parts of the book of Job cannot be translated literally. The translator must first "correct" the mutilated text to intelligible Hebrew before proceeding with his translation. Then we should remember the long line of languages through which our own particular Bible has passed. The Old Testament was written in Hebrew and Aramaic, the New Testament in Greek. Then came a day when Greek was the international language and Hebrew was a dead language. The Old Testament was therefore translated into Greek so that Jews of the Dispersion could understand it in whatever land they lived. Still later, Latin became the language of culture and commerce. The Bible was therefore translated into Latin, still the official language of the Roman Church. As the Church moved across Europe, it continued to read its scripture and its various services in Latin. Christians in Germany dared to believe that Christianity would be more intelligible if presented to the people in language that they understood. In England there was a great need for the Bible in English, but William Tyndale made his Greek translation of the New Testament into English in Germany, not England, in 1525. The men who dared to translate the Bible into English were persecuted, and some of them lost their lives. Their shops were burned, their work stolen or destroyed, and their printing presses smashed. They were excommunicated, pursued to foreign lands, and some of them were burned at the stake. Yet they dared to believe that they were serving God in giving to men the Word of God in language that men could understand.

Still there is work for the translator not only into the remaining languages of mankind at the far ends of the earth; but as new manuscripts, more ancient than those we now possess, come to light, we shall be able to make better translations than have been possible up to now. As long as languages change and words become obsolete or changed in meaning, just so long will the services of the translator be needed. Nevertheless, there are those who would join hands with the inquisitors of old and excommunicate from the Church those who devote themselves to the translation of the Bible into something more intelligible than the King James Version. It is comforting to know that the Church has come to know the Bible not through the inquisitor but through the painstaking work of the man who loved the Bible enough to make it available to others.

The fourth area of biblical scholarship is that of application or interpretation. There are two phases in this area of investigation. First, there is the attempt to be aware of the implications of the writer for the day in which he delivered his message. Too often later developments of thought have intruded upon the picture, and we have read far too much into the words of an earlier day. Second, we seek to discover the application of each particular teaching for our own day. However, in order that we may approach each of these phases of study with the fullest possible understanding, it is necessary to study a third aspect of interpretation. By arranging our biblical materials as nearly as possible in the chronological order of their writing, it will be possible for us to see the steps that man has taken on the way to a discovery of the great truths which we believe are at the heart of religion. Man has had great religious adventures.

Bit by bit he has pieced together his information about the Creator, about the cosmos in which he lives, about his fellow man, about the disturbing or satisfying emotions that enter into his own mind, and about the transitory or permanent nature of the things he feels are important, including his own soul.

The greatest possible value that comes from an intelligent approach to biblical investigation and interpretation is to make a great religious discovery for ourselves. This may more easily come to us as we understand the experiences and processes that led earlier men into their discoveries. As we enter sympathetically into their experiences, we shall be far more likely to accept with approbation the teaching which they have bequeathed to us than if we receive the teaching simply on the basis of authority. How easily men become twisted in their thinking is indicated by the fact that many would seek to prove great truths by the very fact that these truths are in the Bible. Being stated in the Bible does not make a thing true or false. The nature of God did not change because new things were said about him by succeeding generations. God was a God of love long before Hosea discovered that through his own religious experiences, but no one else before Hosea's time had made that discovery. It would be as absurd to say that the world was flat until the discoveries of Copernicus. The universe was not geocentric according to the theories of Ptolemy one day and the next became heliocentric to agree with the pronouncements of Copernicus. The great truths in our Bible are testimony, not to the changing nature of God or our universe, but to the changing mind of man—or put more positively, to the growth of man's understanding of God and creation. It is sobering to admit that all of the more than 250 Protestant denominations in America seek to "prove" their different orthodoxies from the same Bible. Clearly men's experiences are not alike.

It will be my purpose, then, in the succeeding pages to seek to retrace the steps by which man has arrived at some of his greatest convictions, particularly those convictions that later became basic in Christianity. As we undertake these journeys, it is with the hope not only that we shall arrive at an appreciation of the struggles of the mind through which our religious forebears went, but that we shall have an adequate conception of the things in which we believe. If religion is to be meaningful for life, then it must provide guidance and strength for daily living. No mere repetition of the religious discoveries of an earlier generation, no matter how valid those discoveries may have been, will serve to bring religious strength into our lives today. Hearsay religion can save no man.

The great prophets and Jesus were insistent upon the fact that religion is a way of life, and we dare not substitute mechanical performances of religious rites and ceremonies. Too often our Bible study has descended to just that. The daily reading of a stated number of verses or chapters in the Bible is a means of religious strength and guidance only if we learn something that may be applied to life. Unthinking reading of Bible passages can become as mechanical and meaningless as the turning of a prayer wheel in Tibet. To complete the reading of the Bible within a specified number of days cannot be a means of salvation except as such reading brings to us a more intelligent understanding of the process of religion. We must ever remind ourselves that religion cannot be dictated, nor can it be bequeathed: it must be experienced.

The words of Francis Bacon still ring with clarity today, and we shall do well if we respond to their bidding:

I believe that humanity shall accept as an axiom for its conduct the principle for which I laid down my life—the right to investigate. It is the credo of free men—this opportunity to try, this privilege to err, this courage to experiment anew. We scientists of the human spirit shall experiment, experiment, ever experiment. Through centuries of trial and error, through agonies of research . . . let us experiment with laws and customs, with money systems and governments, until we chart the one true course—until we find the majesty of our proper orbit as the planets above have found theirs. . . . And then at last we shall move together in the harmony of our spheres under the impulse of a single creation—one unity, one system, one design.

This insistence upon the right to investigate will perhaps cause some readers to approach old problems from new viewpoints, but that in itself may be a helpful experience and may result in insights never before enjoyed.

3

Priest and Prophet

———◆———

MUCH OF THE OLD TESTAMENT IS CONCERNED WITH THE WORK of prophets and of priests. Much indeed has come to us as a direct result of the writing of both groups. In order that we may fully understand the procession of majestic thinking and see the full stature of the men who blazed the trail, it is necessary to examine the relationships which existed officially or unofficially between priests and prophets. These are the men who made the records of the journey.

Those who are opposed to sacerdotalism see the prophets as the champions of nonliturgical religion and as the natural enemies of the priesthood and all that that group stands for. The thesis that priests and prophets were bitterly opposed to each other has dominated the thinking of too many American scholars, particularly those of the Protestant tradition. A somewhat different position has been taken by British scholarship and by those in Europe.[1] Welch is undoubtedly right when he indicates that the prophets sought a purged cultus, not its elimination.[2] The prophets were wise enough to see that without the regular ministrations of the cultus and the priesthood the lives of the people would be immeasurably poorer. Later abuses in the priesthood led to a wholesome reaction against sacerdotalism, but tragically that reaction has tended to blind us to the good contributed by priestly leadership in Israel.

Before looking at the relationship between priest and prophet, it is necessary to look at the development of the priesthood in

[1] Harper, *Prophetic Element in the Old Testament* (University of Chicago Press, 1905); A. C. Welch, *Prophet and Priest in Old Israel* (London: Student Christian Movement Press, 1936).

[2] *Ibid.*, pp. 10 ff. See also A. R. Johnson, *The Cultic Prophet in Ancient Israel* (Cardiff, Wales: University of Wales Press Board, 1944), p. 6; W. R. Smith. *The Prophets of Israel and Their Place in History* (2nd ed.; New York: The Macmillan Co., 1907), p. 85.

the light of the historical approach to the Old Testament. In the last half of Exodus and in Numbers an ideal picture is given of the priesthood, beginning with the covenant at Mount Sinai, perfectly developed under the leadership of Aaron. Literary analysis has shown that these records come to us in their present form from the fifth century B.C. It is felt by some that such records reflect the conflict that developed in the post-exilic community between the Jerusalem priesthood and the priests of the outlying towns and villages. Be that as it may, it is certainly clear from other sources that in the periods of the patriarchs, of the Judges, and in the early days of the monarchy the structure of the priesthood did not conform to the descriptions in Exodus and Numbers. The Levites had by no means a monopoly of the priesthood.

The well-known story of Gideon shows him functioning at the altar as a priest, and it is clearly stated that he is a Manassite (Judg. 6:15, 19). While it is not stated that Jephthah officiated at the altar in the sacrifice of his daughter, neither does the record indicate that a priest was summoned (Judg. 11:31). Manoah, a Danite, father of Samson, offered a kid with the cereal offering upon the altar; and the sacrifice was miraculously consumed (Judg. 13:19). The story of Micah's son becoming priest because he had "the ephod, and the teraphim, and the graven image" (18:20 K.J.V.) reflects clearly the struggling nature of the priesthood in those days (Judg. 17:7 ff.). Apparently someone discovered that it was good fortune to have a Levite as a priest, and we read of the Danites commandeering for their tribe the services of Micah's priest, a Levite who had been hired instead of the son (Judg. 18:3-5, 19-20).

In the period of the monarchy the priesthood came to be of increasing significance. Yet we do have record of David dancing, evidently as priest, when the ark of the Lord was returned to Israel. As part of the great celebration David also made the sacrifice of an ox on behalf of the people (II Sam. 6:13). Later in his life David offered a special sacrifice to stay a plague, and he built the altar himself at the command of the prophet Gad (II Sam. 24:18-25). No other king dared to function as priest except in the one instance of Saul's proposal for which he was roundly condemned by Samuel (I Sam. 15:17 ff.).

The increasing criticism of the eighth- and seventh-century prophets indicates a deepened moral sensitivity on their part, but it also reflects changes that were coming into the liturgy and priesthood with which the prophets were not in sympathy. It should be noted that the prophets nowhere condemn the priesthood as such, but there is severe criticism that priests are failing to be true leaders of the people. Indeed, it is significant that the prophets are as quick to condemn faithless prophets as they are to criticize disloyal priests. Jeremiah does look forward to the day when priests and symbols will no longer be necessary for the religious instruction of people, but he indicates that they will not be needed because all men will know God and how to commune with him (Jer. 31:34). The prophets sought a purified priesthood and ritual.

The prophets were outspoken on three issues. First, they denounced in no uncertain terms the corruption of the priesthood wherever it was seen, even to charging priests with murder (Hos. 6:9). The list of sins charged against the priests is a formidable one, but it is apparently founded in fact (Hos. 4:6-9; 5:1; Mic. 3:11; Zeph. 3:4). Second, the prophets protested against the increasing emphasis upon liturgical rites and elaborate ceremonies. The constant plea of the prophets that the covenant on Mount Sinai did not establish a sacrificial system reflects the growing movement among the priests to prove that a sacrificial system was established by divine guidance in the desert (Jer. 7:22). Third, and of greatest concern to the prophets was the whole problem of morality in religion. Their protest against ritual was objection not to ritual as such but to the substitution of ritual acts for moral living. They saw the danger that mechanical procedures could be and were being substituted for the spirit of worship grounded in moral conviction (Amos 4:4; 5:22; Hos. 4:13-14; 12:11).

Yet in spite of all these criticisms and revealed weaknesses the priestly system continued to develop and grow. To assume that such growth is due entirely to the machinations and craftiness of the priests is to overlook the fact that priestly religion must have ministered to a felt need in the lives of people. It is seldom that people can be forced to support unwanted services. It must be admitted, however, that many found it easier to follow the mechanical and perhaps financial requirements of a sacri-

ficial system than to respond to the higher moral challenge of
prophetic religion. This was the prophet's concern. He did
not plead for the cessation of ritual but that it should so be
conducted that men would be led to high moral purpose. This
is the dilemma that always faces religious leaders: of building
a system or procedure that will minister to the greatest number, contain challenge for all, and yet carry special significance
for those who are more morally and spiritually sensitive.

During the Exile, and especially in the postexilic period,
leadership shifted among the Jews from political to religious
personnel. Though the term "high priest" was used occasionally
in the preexilic period, it was in the postexilic period that this
office came to its greatest opportunity and responsibility. With
the monarchy gone and the princes serving as representatives
of foreign masters, the people looked more and more to the
high priest as the leader of the spiritual state and the developing
concept of a theocracy. It was during this period that great
literary documents were developed pertaining to the supposed
historical foundations of the priestly and sacrificial system. As
we have noted, this process began before the Exile; but the
record was now considerably enlarged. With emphasis upon
Torah and tradition even greater significance was given to the
priesthood.

It was in this period and in such service that the priest rendered his greatest contribution to the prophetic movement. Tra-
ditionally the priest had been the educator. The content of his
teachings rested upon tradition and included among other
things the teachings of the prophets. The spirit and approach
of the prophet and the priest were very different. The prophet
was usually an impatient individual looking for immediate
change in men and nations. The phrase "Come now, and let us
reason together," (Isa. 1:18) is strange upon the lips of the
prophet. He had no patience with those who failed to catch his
vision. Here was the weakness of the prophet and the place at
which the priest could be of significant service, if not directly
to the prophet, at least to the people whom the prophet failed
to reach. As a teacher the priest knew how to work painstakingly with people, leading them step by step in the direction of
prophetic ideals. Had it not been for the technique of the
teacher stressing "precept upon precept; line upon line" (Isa.

39

28:10 K.J.V.), it is doubtful that prophetic teaching could have made much impact upon men's thinking.

If the teacher was to have materials to present, then certainly there had to be a way of collecting and of copying the materials. This, too, came to be the responsibility of the priesthood. It becomes increasingly clear through literary analysis and historical research that the priests were to a large extent the conservers, compilers, and editors of the biblical record. It has been a major function of religion to conserve the best from the past. This has its dangers, but without it much sacred literature would long since have been lost.

Not only did the priests collect the reported sayings of the prophets, but they organized and edited them. It is altogether possible that the setting of many of the prophetic sayings is in a historical context supplied by later editors, many of whom undoubtedly were priests. But a still more significant change was made in prophetic materials by the priestly group. A quick reading of the prophetic books will show that the messages of the prophets were in many cases adapted for use in a later age than the one in which the prophet spoke. The closing chapters of such books as Amos and Hosea clearly show words of comfort and encouragement which are certainly not the original words of the prophets. Who added them, and why were they added? The words were added in the exilic and postexilic periods because of the new experiences through which the people had gone. Religious teachers in a later age added the new words under the conviction that if the prophets were now living, this is what they would say in these circumstances. Whether or not the prophet would is another question, but the later editors seem to have been motivated by that conviction. Here is a secret of Hebrew-Jewish religion. It was never static. It was always vitally alive. It expressed itself in the light of new situations and new experiences.

Another important editorial service was that of bringing prophetic challenge and legislation together and expressing it in terms of contemporary life. The Deuteronomic reform under Josiah had much prophetic co-operation and inspiration behind it, but it could not have been accomplished without active support from the priesthood. In its later stages the reform may have moved too far in the direction of priestly demand; but at the beginning there seems to have been complete co-operation between political, prophetic, and priestly leadership. In the post-exilic community both Torah and prophetic writings were adapted to the new conditions which obtained. The legislative demands of a desert culture were not nearly as heavy as the demands of an agricultural society after Hebrew entry into Palestine. Complicated sociological problems of the highly organized life in the cities demanded further legislation. With the development of new skills, crafts, and professions still further legislation was demanded. The socio-historical study of Hebrew legislation has clearly revealed the various periods in which legislation was written in response to human necessity. It is significant, also, that when the legislation is arranged in chronological order of its enactment, it is clear that there is a parallel development in the moral conviction behind the changing legislation. This development of moral conviction in turn parallels the challenge presented by the prophetic movement.[3] It now seems clear that the priesthood, which was so definitely a part of the legalistic movement, was responsible for bringing much prophetic idealism into the legislation of the community.

It is doubtful that the priests consciously sought to serve the prophetic movement. Though they were in sympathy with it and drew heavily upon prophetic tradition, they were conscious of their own work and of their responsibility to the people whom they served. Anything else would have been completely unnatural. Prophetic criticism of the priesthood must have stung deeply at times, and it is doubtful that the admiration of the priests for the prophets was deepened through such criticism. There were strained relationships which cannot be overlooked. It is nevertheless true that priest and prophet recognized each other's place in the religious structure. In the chapter "Prophecy as a Profession," pages 45 ff., I shall discuss the place of the prophet in professional leadership. It is necessary here, however, to see some implications of the professional relationship between the two groups.

Each group had its own part to play. There are instances of men being first priests, then becoming prophets (Jer. 1:1; Ezek. 1:3). Hebrew tradition believes that Isaiah also was a priest before becoming a prophet. Still others have been nominated

---

[3] See Chapter Six, "Religion Becomes Moral," pp. 78 ff.

by modern scholarship on the basis that certain prophets seem to know more about the inner working of the cultus than others and seem to be more sympathetic to that cultus. If, as is maintained in the chapter just referred to, the prophet was a recognized member of official religious leadership, then of necessity he must have worked in some official relationship with the priesthood. This in itself would give him an inner knowledge of the cultus and its servants the priests. No theory of special friendship would seem necessary.

Both prophet and priest laid great stress upon the past and glorified history. Their methods of approach to the past were somewhat different. It was the work of the priests to hand on the traditions and to teach them to their own generation. They insisted that the tradition had been handed down through them in unbroken succession. At times either consciously or unconsciously the priests made modern application of ancient laws. Always they had the need of contemporary society in mind. On the other hand, the prophet, arriving at new understandings and insights, tended to project those new ideas into the past and to assume that ancient worthies knew and followed those principles. Even when he announced a principle as an oracle of God revealed through him, he assumed that in an ancient and more perfect day men knew these things but that they had been forgotten and obscured. Now they were being revealed anew.

This difference in approach reflects an essential difference in their work. It was a major task of the prophet to announce oracles from God. It is this task which gives him such standing in the community and with royal and ecclesiastical leadership. If men were to do the bidding of God, as priests and prophets taught, then there must be some means of knowing what the will of God was.[4] One means was through prophetic oracle. Prophets and their contemporaries looked upon such oracles as a special revelation from God to meet specific situations. Though today we may place greater stress upon man's cognitive processes in the unfolding story of religion, it must be recognized that the prophet took no credit for himself but believed that God alone was the source of his knowledge. It was this, and not kinship, that gave the prophet access to kings. The question

[4] See Chapter 10, "God Speaks to Man," pp. 137 ff.

42

of Zedekiah to Jeremiah, "Is there any word from the Lord?" (Jer. 37:77) was not an unusual one but reflects the profound respect that even kings had for the oracle of the prophet.

The work of the priest, on the other hand, centered around knowledge of the tradition. Whether administering the rituals and sacrifices, leading in the stated prayers for various occasions, or engaged in the task of teaching, the priest had to turn to the transmitted information constantly. Anyone who has been associated with the modern counterpart of the priesthood knows the rigidity with which tradition is held. In the morning newspaper is the announcement of a meeting of a group of Roman Catholic clergymen to discuss four hundred years after the death of Martin Luther the advisability of putting more of the liturgy into the current language of the people. Yet such resistance to change has served a very important historical function. It has been the means of preserving for us, frequently in the very words of the past, the things which were believed in an earlier day. This has given us the materials from which we can reconstruct the story of man's growth in religious understanding.

Just as the prophet sought no credit for himself, at least so far as the content of the message was concerned, so the priests were similarly modest. It is seldom that we know the name of a priest, and in almost no case do we know of a priest being credited with the formulation of law. Prophets were concerned about their reputations as spokesmen of God, and priests struggled for ecclesiastical leadership and political power. Both groups were, however, equally modest concerning the possible human origin of religious principles.

In our modern interest in the history of ideas, religious or secular, our curiosity seems to be more fully satisfied if we can point to a precise date or to a specific person as the point of origin for a certain idea. Since in the case of the prophets, their stories are given, as are the messages they uttered, while the priests are left nameless and obscure, it is so much easier to credit the prophets with the discovery of ideas. Rabbi Julian Morgenstern, of Hebrew Union College, credits the prophetic movement with much of the material and many of the concepts to be found in the Pentateuch, though he confesses that in some cases the prophets must remain anonymous.[5] Dr. Immanuel Lewy is more specific. He credits the prophet Nathan with writing "Proto-Samuel," "Proto-Pentateuch," the original Ten Commandments, and other documents. In this he will not be followed by thinking scholarship, but it does show the trend to give personal credit.[6] It is not my purpose to underestimate the importance of the prophets or to discredit their work. I am too well acquainted with their significant place in the history of religion to have anything but the profoundest respect for them and the whole prophetic movement. To glorify the prophets, however, to the disparagement of the priest helps neither the prophet's reputation nor us in our search to understand the historical development of Judaism and its contribution to Christianity. As indicated above, the priestly movement in Israel made its own contribution which was significant and necessary to the development of Hebrew religion.

[5] Paper read to the Society of Biblical Literature, Dec., 1949; see *Journal of Biblical Literature*, LXIX, iv.

[6] *The Birth of the Bible* (New York: Bloch Publishing Co., Inc., 1950).

4

Prophecy as a Profession

———————◆———————

AN ACCEPTED APPROACH TO THE STUDY OF THE PROPHETS ASSUMES
that these men had acknowledged standing in the community
but that they had no particular official relationship to the established organization of religion. Recent studies, particularly a
monograph by Aubrey R. Johnson of South Wales,[1] have drawn
attention to the cultic practices in Canaan and the respective
places of priest and prophet in that culture. Johnson points to
a number of parallels in practice among Hebrew people. It is the
purpose of this chapter to investigate the implications of these
parallels for the history of Hebrew prophecy.

Samuel was the first Hebrew of historical record to be recognized as a prophetic leader. It is important to note that he
functioned also as a priest. In this early period there seems to
be not as clear a differentiation between the two offices as
there was in the succeeding centuries. A more important consideration is the attitude of the people toward the prophet as
he came to the city. Apparently his visit was not in the regular
schedule of things. The people asked, "Is your coming peace-
able?" Could the prophet come in any other way? The people's
question implies that he could; for when he answered, "Yes,"
the community was content and bid him welcome (I Sam.
16:4-5. Cf. I Sam. 7:5-12). The right of the prophet to bring
a message of blessing or of cursing is recognized by Johnson [2]
and seems to be well attested from the ancient record. This
seems to move beyond the place of being merely a word of praise
or censure. Nor was it confined to prediction of coming events,
good or ill. Rather it bore to the community the conviction that
it was being blessed or punished by God through the prophet

[1] *Op. cit.*
[2] *Ibid.*, p. 40.

45

right then. The blessing or cursing may not immediately be apparent, but the word had been uttered.

Samuel functioned in three capacities—that of priest, that of seer or prophet, and that of judge. It is not always clear in what department he was functioning in every case. Apparently there was yet no clear distinction between these several offices, or at least it was considered that the same individual was capable of serving in each capacity. At a later date there was a substitution of the monarchy for the office of judge. Participation in altar rites was reserved to the priesthood. Utterance of the oracles of God came to be the special responsibility of the prophet. In Chapter Three we were concerned with the special problems that center around the relationship of priest and prophet. It is needful here to recognize only that Samuel did serve in both capacities. In each of them he was a recognized member of the official religious leadership. He did not step outside it when he functioned as a prophet and reenter it when he served as a priest.

Whether the people recognized any differentiation of office at that time is not clear. It is true that in a later period only first-born sons in the Levitical tribe could qualify as priests, but that did not stop their functioning as prophets. Men could, however, be prophets even though they were not qualified to be priests. The question arises, Was the priest a professional religious leader and the prophet nonprofessional? What constitutes professional leadership?

In the religious field the term "professional" is sometimes used in an invidious sense. It is not so used here. By "professional" is meant an officially accredited person who serves within the framework of the organized religious group. Several tests may be applied. (1) Usually the profession demands special training or capabilities. (2) Services rendered have recognition through financial or other recompense. (3) Provision is made in the cultic pattern for the proper exercise of such professional leadership. (4) There is recognition by related officers of the same religious organization. Let us look at each of these in turn.

1. Special training and adequate qualifications were expected of the man who would be a prophet. There is record of at least four prophets setting up organizations of followers presumably

46

for the purpose of training. Samuel is the recognized head of a prophetic group (I Sam. 19:20), and Isaiah refers more than once to his followers (Isa. 8:16; 36:8). Elisha was the successor of Elijah whether trained by him or not. His leadership of the prophetic group was immediately recognized, and the group came to him immediately after the passing of Elijah (II Kings 2:15 ff.). As has been pointed out frequently, the term "sons of the prophets" had no reference to genealogy but indicated the special group of functioning prophets.

Qualifications involved several things. First, the established pattern seems to have been to announce one's call to prophecy through the relating of a vision from God. Isaiah's vision in the Temple, Amos' vision of the basket of summer fruit, Ezekiel's strange vision of the four-faced, four-winged creature, are but a few examples. It is well to note here contrary to some writers that the prophet received his initial call to prophecy through a vision but did not necessarily believe that all his insights would come to him through visions.[3] Second, the prophet had to have poetic ability. His messages had to be couched in metrical form and chanted at the stated festivals of the Hebrew religion. Even Amos, who stands outside the regular pattern of prophetic leadership by his own request, nevertheless had to meet this standard if his message was to be heard. The result is that Amos has given us what is undoubtedly some of the best Hebrew poetry. As I indicate elsewhere,[4] a major reason for the careful preservation of the prophetic word was its literary quality. Third, and this seems not always to have been demanded, members of the prophetic group had to have skill in penmanship. They were the writers of the community. Our Bible makes reference to the records kept by the prophets, records from which some of our biblical materials were drawn (see I Chron. 29:26-29).

2. How fully the prophetic order was supported financially by the community, we have no way of knowing. There is record of some recompense, however. When Saul planned to avail him-

[3] Cf. John Skinner, *Prophecy and Religion* (New York: The Macmillan Co., 1936), pp. 10 ff.

[4] See my "Literature of the Old Testament" in an annotated edition of *The Bible, An American Translation,* to be published by the University of Chicago Press.

self of the services of Samuel his servant named what presumably would be an acceptable fee (I Sam. 9:7-10). If this reference is in terms of coinage, then of course it is a late addition to the story; but it still reflects the attitude of the late community toward the prophets. When Amos appeared in Bethel, he was warned to leave immediately and to seek recompense for his messages in Jerusalem (Amos 7:12-13). Here is clear evidence that financial reward of some kind was practiced. Of course it may be objected that charlatans are also paid and are not officially recognized members of a profession, but such charlatans can collect only through deception or because they offer their services more attractively or more reasonably than the regular members of the profession. We shall recognize that recompense does not necessarily prove that one belongs to the profession, but it does show that society is willing to pay for such services as if they were professional.

3. Members of the prophetic order were expected to function within the established procedures of the group and of society. Even free-lance prophets who expected to have a hearing had of necessity to meet the generally accepted standards. We turn again to Amos, for here was a religious rebel who was certainly not a part of any professional group. Yet if Amos was to be heard, he could be heard only as he prepared himself to participate in the established patterns. At the time of the great festival at Bethel opportunity was given to men who were under the conviction of God to speak whether they were members of the prophetic guild or not.

Not only did Amos carefully phrase his messages in the choicest of poetry, but he delivered them at the appointed time. Here was no uncouth farm hand rudely interrupting a formal religious service by striding belligerently down the aisle to hurl his denunciations upon a startled congregation. His denunciations were no less fierce because he did conform to pattern, but conform he did. Otherwise he may not have been heard. This does not mean that Amos compromised. It merely means that he was acquainted with established procedures and knew that he could obtain his best hearing if he met the conditions. If a confessed nonmember of the prophetic guild felt the pressure of the group procedure, it is an indication of the rigidity with which the pattern had been established. It indicates, if not a full official place in the cultic pattern, at least a fully approved status in the community. It must be noted, however, that once a man had established his reputation, then it was possible to deliver messages at any time by appearing in the precincts of the Temple, in the market place, or other public assemblies.

4. Recognition by others in the official structure is an important piece of evidence in establishing the relationship of prophecy to the total religious organization. No question can be raised concerning the official status of the priesthood, for many detailed passages are given over to the legislation concerning their place in organized religion. From the descriptions it would appear that the priests would be empowered and qualified to take care of any religious need that could arise in the lives of people. When, however, priestly records make specific place for other religious functionaries, it is significant. Professions do not ordinarily make place for free-lance individuals to assume certain prerogatives within an established craft. Recognition by the priesthood, therefore, must mean an official status of some kind. The book of Deuteronomy immediately after its treatment of the Levitical priesthood and a brief statement on divination turns then to a discussion and treatment of prophecy (18:1-22). Such a setting would seem to justify our assumption that both priest and prophet were considered regular functionaries in the official structure of religion. The linking of the terms "priest" and "prophet" in prophetic and other writings would similarly support the same assumption. The book of Lamentations would even place both in the Temple (2:20).

Perhaps one other aspect may be considered here. There is much conflict evidenced in the record between the so-called true and false prophets. The greatest moments of clash come between the prophets of Yahweh and those of other religions. Elijah meets with representatives of Baalism on Mount Carmel; and the statement is clear that such prophets "eat at Jezebel's table" (I Kings 18:19), that is, they receive their support in the royal household. Similarly, the conflict of opinion between Micaiah, son of Imlah, and the prophets of the royal household seems to indicate that the latter were gainfully employed as prophets (I Kings 22:6-8). It would seem incongruous, therefore, that though the prophets of Yahweh should oppose the prophets of other religions, they would so deviate from established pattern that they received no recompense and had no official standing within their own cultus.

The prophets of Yahweh, as indicated by the evidence, not only had standing in the community but had official acceptance and standing within the cultic pattern. It would seem, therefore, that these men would of necessity have special responsibilities which other men could not assume. One immediately thinks of the oracles which came from the prophets. Down to the period of the Babylonian exile there was clear recognition of this special responsibility of the prophets. In the postexilic period it is assumed that all oracles had been delivered in early times. It is sometimes affirmed that the priesthood displaced the prophets in the postexilic community. The sequence of events is not in such sharp succession. With the discovery of the Law in the Temple in 621 B.C. an emphasis came upon the written documents such as had never been known before. Now the spirit of religion was "thus it is written," whereas it had been "thus saith the Lord." With the importance of a written document recognized, religion then needed readers, copyists, and interpreters. The priests were qualified and anxious to accept such tasks. The written document had displaced the spoken word, and the natural result was for the priest to be of increasing significance, and the prophets therefore dropped into insignificance. There was another flurry of the old spirit in a later age, a movement known to us as apocalypticism. Its spirit was, however, greatly different from that of the old prophets, and it is unfortunate that dictionary definitions and popular definitions of prophecy are so frequently in terms of apocalypticism and not true prophecy.

There is another aspect of prophetic activity, however, which has not been fully recognized. The prophets were intimately related to God and history. As William A. Irwin has indicated,[5] the prophets were among the earliest to recognize the continuity of history. They saw the future as an outgrowth of the present. Man's present conduct determined what would happen to him in the future. God was not a god of caprice. Events in the world were explainable in terms of law and of order. To be sure, God had a purpose for history and for mankind; but all events

[5] *Old Testament: Keystone of Human Culture* (New York: Henry Schuman, Inc., 1952), pp. 161 ff.

had not been foreordained. The end purpose of life was established, and God was constantly working with men to bring them into harmony with his purposes and to bring them to such quality of life that he could use them in the accomplishment of his great purposes.

There were therefore two things that the prophets could do. The first has been fully recognized. It was their task to teach men, to warn them, and to persuade them to bring their lives into harmony with the will of God. The second is a little more obscure. What if men would not heed their messages? Did the prophets fold their hands with the feeling that at least they had delivered their own souls? Not at all. There was the message of condemnation, but at times there was activity on the part of the prophets that indicates that they were using techniques to help God bring punishment upon men. It was a type of mimetic, or imitative, magic. Perhaps this is why the prophet was so much feared at times.

The prophet's use of imitative magic could be used for the people's weal or woe, but always in harmony with what he believed to be the purposes of God. Elijah on Mount Carmel sought to demonstrate that Yahweh, the supposed god of the desert, was also the god of natural agricultural processes. Rain could be sent by Yahweh, but the people believed that this was Baal's function. The original story centered about an answer by rain, not by fire.[6] To induce the coming of rain, Elijah used mimetic magic. He poured water out as a sign of the coming of rain, not as a guarantee against deception on his part. Still later, as a cloud moved in from the Mediterranean, Elijah ran rapidly along the valley of Jezreel. A natural interpretation in the thought is that Elijah was guiding the fructifying rain along the valley which so much needed it. Our concern at the moment is not with historicity or with the logic of this account but with its insight into the thought patterns of the ninth century B.C. (I Kings 18:33-35).

A revealing record is given to us in the annals of Elisha (II Kings 13:14-19). The dying prophet was visited by King Joash. Under the guidance of the prophet the king shot an arrow from the window, but not before the prophet touched his tensed

---

[6] See my article in *American Journal of Semitic Languages*, LI (July, 1935), 233 ff. See also pp. 61 ff below.

hands. The specially directed arrow because of the word and action of the prophet ensured victory for Joash over the Syrians in Aphek. Then the king was instructed to take arrows and beat them upon the ground. The king did so; but when he struck the ground only three times, Elisha was incensed. Had the king struck the ground more often under the direction of the prophet, more victories would have been forthcoming. The prophet said, "Now you will strike down Syria only three times" (v. 19 R.S.V.). We can agree with Johnson that here is a clear case of a prophet's use of mimetic magic.[7] The term "theurgy" is perhaps to be preferred, for these prophets had no intention of manipulating Deity for man's ends. Rather their emphasis was upon aiding God in his purposes. The term "magic" used here designates technique, not religious point of view as in Chapter 7.

In the sixth century B.C. there were several instances of similar pattern. Jeremiah's controversy with Hananiah and his use of first a wood then an iron yoke is best understood not as an illustrated sermon but as the prophet's use of mimetic magic. Jeremiah was literally putting his country under the yoke of captivity, but Hananiah broke the power of his message by smashing the wood yoke. Jeremiah returned to the fray with a yoke of iron, and Hananiah was powerless to defeat Jeremiah (Jer. 27:2; 28:2-3, 10, 13). Perhaps the smashing of the clay pot in chapter 19 is a similar pattern.

Ezekiel in the same period condemned in no uncertain terms the women who used imitative magic to cast spells and cause deaths (Ezek. 13:17-23), but he himself did not hesitate to make use of the ancient techniques. He was convinced not only that the city of Jerusalem was doomed but that it must fall in accord with the will of God and as a punishment to the sinning Hebrew people. When word finally did come through to Babylon that Jerusalem had fallen, Ezekiel was as disturbed and distressed as anyone. Nevertheless, he had not hesitated to use the force of his office to help God accomplish the downfall of the city. Ezekiel therefore inscribed a map of Jerusalem upon a clay tablet, set up seige against it, and went through a demonstration of mock warfare and seige (Ezek. 4:1-3). No adequate explanation is found for the prophet's actions except in terms

[7] *Op. cit.*, p. 37.

of imitative magic. Illustrated sermons were not in fashion, and the Hebrew captives did not need to be reminded that their beloved city was being beseiged. Ezekiel's message was one of doom, not of hope; and the people believed that it carried not only conviction but accomplishment with it. It may be objected that the next story in Ezekiel is scarcely possible of physical accomplishment, lying on one's side for 390 days. We agree, but it must be recognized that each story in Ezekiel must be examined by itself, for throughout the book there is a variety of types of illustration, some of which are only literary device. The story of the mock seige fits so perfectly the pattern of Semitic imitative magic that this makes the most logical explanation.

A book which has caused much concern is Nahum. Two major questions have been raised concerning it. First, was it written before or after the fall of Nineveh? Second, since there is almost no religious message in the book, why is it included among the prophetic books? Let us look at the second question first. The opening chapter, as indicated by its acrostic structure, was written much later than the rest of the book. The acrostic introduction probably means that the book was adapted to Temple liturgy and worship. This heightens the question of the content of the rest of the book. Is it possible to see in this book another instance of the use of mimetic magic? At the time of the attack upon the city of Nineveh a singer may have been persuaded to sing the doom of the city. When the news came of the actual fall of Nineveh, it would have been well within the thought pattern of that day to credit the singer with at least an "assist." The book was remembered because it had been written at the pending fall of Nineveh and the city had fallen. In a later age, when emphasis was upon the power of prediction, the book had even further significance.

It may also have been used in still another way. Just as the book of Esther has been used to express enmity for many enemies of Judaism, so this book was specially prepared for Temple use with its acrostic introduction. It could then be used, if not as powerful magic, at least in wishful thinking that another enemy was marked for destruction. Apart from the howl of glee that the enemy city has fallen, there is little in the book of Nahum; but at least it is now more understandable as a sample of men's thinking in an earlier day. The question of the date is automatically resolved. By this interpretation the book must have been written immediately before the fall of Nineveh in 612 B.C.

Two other aspects of the prophet's work need to be examined as indications of his professional standing. From the days of the origin of the Hebrew monarchy onward, the prophetic group either assumed or had given to it the responsibility of seeing that the right men became monarchs. In the early days the law of primogeniture had not determined the right of succession to the throne. In more than one instance councils or intrigue, perhaps both, determined the succession. The advice of the prophet played no small part in the final decision. It was the prophet Nathan who interviewed the dying David and obtained the decree that Solomon, not Adonijah, should succeed to the throne (I Kings 1:11-14, 22-31).

It was the prophet Elisha who selected one of the band of prophets, gave him the anointing oil, and sent him to anoint Jehu at Ramoth-gilead. The act signalized a coup d'état and the end of the house of Ahab. Although presumably the anointing was done in the privacy of another room, when it became known that Jehu had thus been selected by a prophet, who remains anonymous, the military leaders immediately hailed their new king. No question is raised concerning the right of the prophet to do this deed. Of course it is perfectly obvious that the assumed innocency of Jehu is part of the proceedings. All has been carefully planned, and it seems most likely that the military leaders knew what had been planned. However, it was the admission of an anointing by a prophet that was the climax of the episode. Only if the prophet had official standing in the religious cultus, could such an act be possible. Otherwise there would be chaos. Any conniving political upstart could arrange to have a so-called prophet anoint him unless there was some control by society.

It is apparent that the prophets were definitely involved in politics. It was their responsibility to see that the right political leadership was in power. By right political leadership they meant leaders who were in sympathy with and if possible loyal members of Yahweh religion as taught and expressed by the prophets. Careful examination of the political history of Israel and Judah reveals the active and important participation of the prophets. It is altogether possible that the sudden demise of Amon and the succession of the boy king Josiah had the full approval, if not guidance, of the prophetic party. The careful coaching of the king in the thought patterns of Yahwism immediately prior to the discovery of the scroll of law in the Temple is more than coincidence. The prophetic party was now back in its rightful place of spiritual counselor and guardian of God's people.

Continuity of the prophetic community is indicated in a number of instances, though the picture is far from clear. We have already noted the group of followers gathered around Isaiah. Sigmund Mowinckel has demonstrated through traditio-historical criticism the importance of the prophetic community in the transmission and shaping of prophetic utterances. He says:

> The Isaiah circle whose existence is proved by the sources, and whose marks can be traced through the post-Isaian prophecy, has continued up to Deutero-Isaiah and his time and posterity. In reality, this means that Deutero-Isaiah has sprung from the Isaiah circle and has marked it for posterity with his spirit. That also explains the fact which has provoked so many unanswered questions, namely, that the sayings of Deutero-Isaiah and his successors ("Trito-Isaiah") have been transmitted as an appendix to the book of Isaiah.[8]

How the prophets arrived at their messages is discussed in Chapter Fourteen.[9] In Part Two we shall be concerned specifically with a number of the significant contributions by the prophets to religious thinking. The utterance of the message of the prophet was his most important task, yet it will help us to understand those messages if we understand the prophet as a person. It is hoped that these paragraphs will give a fuller and truer picture of the prophets than has been possible heretofore. The prophets usually were not lone individuals working independently of organized religion. They were recognized

[8] *Prophecy and Tradition* (Oslo, Norway: Jacob Dybwad, 1946), p. 46: *Profetien fra Jesaja til Jeremia* (Oslo, Norway: Jacob Dybwad, 1926).

[9] Pp. 185 ff.

members of the religious organization. They met specific requirements of office. Frequently they had support from the group, though the individuality of their messages led often to criticism, often to loneliness, and sometimes to ostracism from the group. They played a very important part in the structure of the community; and while in many cases the impact of their messages was not felt for many generations, yet there was specific action, particularly in the political arena, that had far-reaching results. The ultimate importance of the prophetic messages has been fully recognized. The immediate results of the work of the prophets as working members of the religious organization is only now beginning to be understood.

PART TWO

The Procession of Majestic Thinking

5

Man Discovers God

STUDENTS OF COMPARATIVE RELIGION AFFIRM THAT NO GROUP of people has been found anywhere which has not believed in some form of divine power. There may be an occasional individual who is without such thought, but communities of atheists do not exist except as they are artificially organized. The more primitive people are, the simpler are their concepts of deity. The belief in one God (monotheism) is a highly developed concept, possible only after man has done some intense thinking about the world in which he finds himself. Early man believed that there were many gods, each god having some specific duty or phase of nature with which he was associated. Some were good forces, some were evil.

Man believed that there was a constant struggle in nature between the forces of good and the forces of evil, and he saw the struggle evidenced year by year in the procession of the seasons. Each fall the sun god ripened the grain, but he also killed vegetation. All trees and plant life were dead during the winter months. The days increased in warmth and length as the good gods were winning and decreased as the evil forces gained control. Man quite naturally assumed that the forces of good were on his side and the forces of evil were associated with his political enemies. Man believed that through magic he could persuade the gods to do his bidding, and that by offering gifts he could make them well disposed toward him. The pictures are sometimes crude, but nonetheless they greatly influenced the patterns of man's conduct.

From the oldest records of the Hebrews it is clear that they were far from being a people who believed in only one god. It shall not be attempted here to trace their experiences through the stages of animism, supposed totemism, ancestor worship, and similar early patterns of thinking. Our purposes necessitate only that we shall recognize the crude patterns of their early religious beliefs and then move on quickly to see the development of ethical monotheism, the most magnificent contribution by the Hebrews to world thinking.

Much has been written concerning the contribution of Moses as a religious leader of the Hebrew people. It is not the purpose here to enter into debate concerning the sources of Moses' ideas of God. It has been indicated that the Egyptians, the Kenites, and the Phoenicians were the first people to know God as *one* God, and that Moses was taught by them and then carried the idea to the Hebrews. There is no evidence that any of these people had a true monotheism. All of them believed in many deities, gods in their own land and gods of other people. It has been reported by Charles Virolleaud that the name YHWH (Yahweh) appears on tablets found at Ras Shamra (ancient Ugarit) coming from the fourteenth century B.C.[1] If this is true, then it is the earliest known use of the name by which the Hebrews knew God; and it will necessitate a revision of many theories concerning the origin of Israel's religion. It must, however, be noted this does not mean that monotheism was a belief of the Ugaritans or any other people in that region. Other tablets from that same place and period list a multitude of other gods in whom the people believed.

Was Moses a monotheist? There is much evidence that he was not, but there is every indication that he did believe that his followers should themselves worship only Yahweh, the God of the Hebrews. Neither he nor they, however, denied the existence of the gods of other peoples. Such a position is not monotheism; it is henotheism or monolatry. Monotheism is

[1] *La Déesse 'Anat* (Paris: P. Geuthner, 1938) , p. 98. See also Rowley, *op. cit.*, pp. 148 ff.

the belief that there is only one divine power. None other exists. Henotheism is the belief in a supreme power for a particular national or tribal group but does not claim that no other divine power exists. A failure to use terms correctly has led to much confusion in their area. Moses may be called the father of Hebrew religion, and his work was essential to the later developments in religious thinking, but the Hebrews did not arrive at monotheism until many centuries after the death of Moses. It is well to confess, therefore, that since Moses was not a monotheist, there is little point to debating whether or not the Egyptians or the Kenites gave Moses his monotheistic concepts.

We likewise should like to know the significance of the personal name (YHWH) by which Moses came to know God (see Exod. 3:13-14). Many suggestions have been made. Most of them have revolved around the concept of "existence" and the verb "to be." Some ingenious proposals have been made based upon other etymologies.[2] But it should be remembered that an abstract concept of existence is not likely to be held by early tribesmen wandering in a desert, nor is it probable that Moses could have secured a following for a new God on such a basis. The meaning of the name has been lost, and we have no satisfactory solution to offer except that the name must have conveyed the idea that this God of Moses had the power to lead the people victoriously from slavery to freedom. In any case the religious banner under which Moses marshaled his forces was a banner destined to have world-wide recognition. One God for a tribe or federation of tribes was a necessary concept on the way to a belief in one God for one world. To Moses belongs the glory for having taken his people that far on the great journey of the discovery of that one God.

Other records indicate that the early Hebrews were far removed from monotheism. Recall, for example, the experience of the Hebrews during one of Moses' visits to the mount of God. In Exod. 32:1 ff. there is the familiar account of the golden calf. Moses had been gone from camp for a long time,

---

[2] R. A. Bowman, "Yahweh, the Speaker," *Journal of Near Eastern Studies,* III (Jan., 1944), 1-8; James A. Montgomery, "The Hebrew Divine Names and the Personal Pronoun HU," *Journal of Biblical Literature,* LXIII, No. 2 (June, 1944), 161 ff.

and the people were uneasy. They had left Egypt under the leadership of this man Moses, who alone had communed with the Deity by whom they were being led; and now this leadership was gone. In despair the people turned to Aaron, who ordered them to contribute the gold of their ornaments. The metal was poured into a mold having the shape of a bull. We may ask, Why a bull? We may also be curious concerning the presence of such a mold in the camp. Undoubtedly the mold and the idea of a bull-god were both carried from Egypt. The bull-god Apis must have been perfectly familiar to the Hebrews during their sojourn in Egypt. The bull-god was well known throughout the Near and Middle East. It was known by various names, but most frequently in our Bible as Baal. Aaron called the new image a god, "who brought you up out of the land of Egypt" (Exod. 32:4). If, as is thought by some scholars, this story was revived many years later during the bitter fight against Baal worship, it only serves to show how strong and how late that religion had importance in the mind of the Hebrew people.

Another familiar story is that of Gideon, who was a champion of the Yahweh religion (Judg. 6:24 ff.). Yet as we read the account, we become aware of the fact that Gideon lived in a home and in a town where Baalism was the official religion. The story is delightfully told by a skillful artist. Gideon was under conviction that he must destroy the altar of Baal, cut down the symbolic pole that was beside the altar, and sacrifice to Yahweh the fat bull that had been saved for years by his family for a noble sacrifice to Baal. Gideon was temporarily delayed by fear; and what he feared to do in daylight, he accomplished under cover of darkness. His deed was discovered at daybreak, and investigation quickly revealed that he was the perpetrator of the awful deed. The death penalty was called for with a full expectation on the part of the townspeople that Gideon would pay for his crime. The fact that they could ask for his life was an indication that Baalism was the all-important religion in that community. Gideon's father made clever defense, saying, in effect, "If Baal is a God, let him plead his own case." In any event the life of Gideon was spared, but there is no indication that the community denied the existence of Baal.

Careful examination of many ancient temples and of their rituals indicates that people believed in many gods and that these gods were associated with different lands, with different cities, or perhaps with different functions of nature. Long after the Hebrews came into the land of Palestine, they associated Yahweh with the desert. He was the god of battle and of storm, and was normally thought to dwell in the mountains. As they settled in the land of Canaan, they learned that the god Baal was believed to be the god of vegetation and productivity. What was more natural, then, than that they should seek the aid of Baal in their agricultural pursuits, still reserving the right to call on Yahweh when they needed help in battle. But what of those who believed that the Hebrews owed allegiance to Yahweh alone? There seem to have been no defenders of this position, at least none who were vocal in that day, with the exception of Elijah (I Kings 18:1 ff.).

That was a strange contest on Mount Carmel. Four hundred and fifty against one man. Not only was that one man led to victory by his god on that day, but history has accorded him a place among the glorious, while the 450 have lost all identity and are known only as those defeated by Elijah. In recent years because of the almost endless investigation by students of Semitic culture and the tireless spadework of archaeologists the significance of the contest is now more apparent. It was a clash of cultures, a struggle of religious patterns.

On the one side was the one defendant of Israel's ancient religious culture. At least this was his belief. Actually he had thought his way to newer and higher levels of religious thinking. Then like so many of his successors he projected them into the past and cried, "Let us return to the good old ways!"

On the other side of the contest were religious men who had learned the necessary techniques of their religion, techniques that had taken shape through the centuries and had been firmly fixed in the culture of that day. This religion was almost completely concerned with the material prosperity of its adherents, people who were an agricultural people and who therefore were vitally concerned that crops should grow and that herds should increase. They believed that they had discovered this way through religion, a religion that rested back upon magic as its main tool. They believed that out of the love life of the gods came the fructification of their fields and animals, and the magical approach was to enact such scenes upon earth as would cajole or magically impel the gods to give the increase. Much of their technique centered in the necessity of bringing to life year by year the god (or Baal) of fertility. Yearly he died with the crops, and year by year he was restored to life through the incantations of the faithful.

The people who came to make up the Hebrew nation had come in from the desert. Their life had been in tents, black goats-hair tents. Life had been harsh and hard, a desert culture. Now they were in the land of "milk and honey," but they soon discovered that they had to wrest a living from the soil. They were now farmers. As they changed from wanderers of the desert to agriculturists, new methods had to be learned; and as soon as they were on speaking terms with their neighbors, they borrowed tools, customs, and habits. What was more natural than that they would also turn to the religion of their neighbors, particularly since the Israelites associated their tribal deities with the desert, and this new religion of Canaan was thought to be especially good for farmers. As time passed, more and more of the Hebrews were becoming adherents of the religion of the Baal. To a champion of the traditional religion of Israel a clash was inevitable.

Perhaps even more dangerous than a complete change-over by many of the people to the religion of Baal was the confusion of thinking and the fusion of ideology on the part of large numbers of the people. They used the old terminology, but they had new patterns of thought. Elijah could not be expected in that day to know that he had a problem of syncretism on his hands. For him the issue was clear-cut, "Choose today whom you will serve" (Josh. 24:15). It was either Yahweh or Baal. So the issue was drawn. On the one side was Elijah, champion of Yahweh; on the other, the prophets of Baal. The people were not innocent bystanders. The issue was not theological abstraction, but it meant a changed way of life if the decision went against them. For the most part they were on the side of the religion of the land, Baalism.

The record has been somewhat obscured by later insertions to magnify supernatural abilities of the "prophet of the Lord." It is clear, however, that the prophets of Baal were in political favor in that day, because of the fanatical zeal of Jezebel for her own religion and the spineless attitude of her husband toward the religion of his fathers. Because of this defection on the part of the political leaders of Israel, Elijah had denounced Ahab as the real "troubler of Israel." He believed that through divine intervention summoned by Elijah himself there was a three-year drought. In fact the main issue on Mount Carmel was that a choice should be made on the basis of which God should give an answer by rain. Elijah was quite certain that just as God had withheld the rain at his behest, so the rain could return in answer to his prayers.

Elijah stood before the people and challenged them to make a choice: "If the Lord be God, follow him: but if Baal, then follow him" (I Kings 18:21). No one dared to commit himself. Again the prophet spoke:

I, even I only, am left as a prophet of the Lord, but the prophets of the Baal are four hundred and fifty men. Let them therefore give us two bulls, and let them choose one bull for themselves and cut it in pieces and lay it on the wood but make no fire, and I will prepare the other bull and place it on the wood, but I will make no fire. Then call you on the name of your god and I will call on the name of the Lord; and the god who answers by fire, *he is God* (italics mine). (I Kings 18:22-24.)

The people answered, "It is a fair test!" and the test began.

The prophets of Baal prepared their sacrifice and began their regular ritual. From morning until noon they prayed, "O Baal, answer us." But there was not even a sound. How weary they must have been! They were physically weary from the peculiar limping dance that was part of their religious technique and mentally weary from the strain of the test, but no answer came to their cries.

Now Elijah began to mock them. He was thoroughly familiar with their methods and beliefs. He knew that many of them must have believed that the test was useless, for this was not the season in which their god could answer. It was the regular time in the cycle of yearly events in which the god was in the midst of his winter sleep, on that journey which year by year he took down under the world after the harvesting of grain. No wonder Elijah said, in effect, "Shout! You need to wake him up, to bring him back from that long journey." He knew as well as they that the time for that prayer was only at the spring festival.

Imagine believing in a god who was the servant and not the master of the seasons. But the prophets of Baal had everything at stake, so they renewed their pleas and intensified their activities. Not only did they shout out their pleas, but they slashed themselves with knives, pouring out their own blood in a type of self-sacrifice. What shall we say of the sincerity of the religion of a man that will take him to such extremes? The sincerity of these men was not in question. Their fault was that of false thinking, of believing that material prosperity came in direct proportion to the correctness of method used to inveigle God to do man's bidding.

Man later learned to pray, "Not my will, but thine, be done" (Luke 22:42 K.J.V.). It is easier, however, to condemn men as being insincere than it is to teach them to think correctly or even to see the false steps by which they arrived at their present convictions. The failure to understand the enormity of this problem is well illustrated by that choir leader who, when he comes to this section of the *Elijah*, dances lightly by as though this were a pastorale, a reverie beside still waters. Instead, there were 450 men beside themselves with disappointment. Four hundred fifty men shouting their prayers, cutting themselves until blood gushed out. It can be expressed only by full choir in double forte, with full support from the organ, every sixteen-foot stop pulled out and with pedal crescendo. Baal must awake! But he didn't.

As Elijah turned to the altar that he had erected, the people must have felt the tremendous contrast. The confidence of quiet action. The time of noise had gone by, but there was a feeling of even greater tension. To us it may seem strange that Elijah at such a moment as that could even be guilty of descending to magical techniques. Yet it is not strange, for he was a child of his own day and must be judged in the light of the knowledge and even of the moral levels of that day. He could not be expected to have the knowledge that was available to men who lived centuries after him. He turned to the altar and caused water to be poured out three times over the sacrifice. It has usually been assumed that this was done in order that there might be no reason to suspect deception. It undoubtedly had that effect; but there is the probability, as was noted in Chapter Four, that Elijah was using magical incantation. By pouring out the water he was enacting the coming of rain. Similar rites are known to us from the surrounding cultures. There may be some significance too in the fact that it was done three times, three being a holy number. The reference to four containers of water is undoubtedly a later insertion; four containers emptied three times might represent the twelve tribes.

As we turn to the verses (I Kings 18:36-37) giving the prayer of Elijah and the answer, we face the difficulty of disagreement of the versions. The record is far from clear, but we can trust tradition that Elijah and the people were conscious of an answer from Yahweh. The people cried, "The Lord, he is God; the Lord, he is God." After disposing of the prophets of Baal, Elijah turned to Ahab with the important assertion, "Go up, eat and drink; for there is the rushing sound of rain."

While Ahab was taking care of what may have been a ceremonial feast of thanksgiving, Elijah went back up Mount Carmel. In this act we have revealed the tremendous tension under which he was working. So confident was he that his prayer had been answered that he had already announced to the king the coming of rain. Yet while the king feasted, Elijah was crouched to the ground, his face between his knees (I Kings 18:42), not daring to look for the answer to his own prayer. Instead, he sent his servant to gaze out over the Mediterranean, for it was from that direction that the rain clouds must come. Six times the servant was sent, and six times he returned with the same answer, "There is nothing." Still that man crouched to the ground when others would have given up in despair long ago. What kept him there, and what persuaded him to send his servant once again to look out to sea?

Here is interesting material for the student of the psychology of prayer. The faith of the man in his announcement to Ahab and in his sending the servant repeatedly to gaze seaward seemed not to be in agreement with his own conduct as expressed in his physical actions. It is the same tension that many a man has experienced in his prayer life. He is sure, and yet— Suddenly the servant returned with the answer for which Elijah had waited so long. "There is a cloud the size of a man's hand, rising out of the sea." What an anticlimax! That was far from being a storm cloud. It was enough for Elijah. Immediately he sent word to Ahab that if he wanted to get home without having his horses bogged down in the mud, he should start immediately. The king may have objected, that the countryside was burned dry after three years without rain. But Elijah was not a man to be trifled with. Down the valley of Jezreel raced the horses of Ahab. Meantime the heavens grew black with storm. The most amazing spectacle was Elijah himself running ahead of the horses, another indication of his tension. Under ordinary circumstances it could not be expected that Elijah or anyone else could run so far or so fast. Psychologists attest to the fact that under times of strain and stress feats comparable to this are by no means unknown to man. Perhaps this Hebrew writer was trying to indicate the unusualness of this act of Elijah's when he recorded, "The hand of the Lord also was on Elijah so that he girded up his loins and ran before Ahab to the entrance of Jezreel" (I Kings 18:46) .[3]

Reaction set in immediately. Jezebel was not so easily disposed of. Her prophets may have been slain, but she was still queen in Israel. A messenger was sent to Elijah informing him that Queen Jezebel had sworn an oath to take his life. The effect was immediate. Elijah was changed from a man of conquest to a defeated, dejected runaway. A change as sudden as this one must have been prompted by unusual circumstances. At least two are outstanding and worthy of our consideration. The first was Jezebel the queen. She was a woman who could by no means be trusted. She allowed nothing to thwart her purposes. The second was normal physiological reaction of mind and body. Worn with the struggle, Elijah fled to Mount Horeb. He was temporarily defeated. Nevertheless he had won an amazing victory, one that undoubtedly contributed to the final triumph of Yahweh over Baal. Yet it should again be noted that the people of that day believed it to be a real struggle between opposing gods. The Hebrews had not yet arrived at monotheism.

The bitterness of the struggle between Yahwism and Baalism is only now becoming clear. Every archaeological excavation in Palestine bears testimony to the tremendous hold which this religion had upon that land. The struggle is reflected also in

[3] See p. 51 above.

the words of the prophets who were Baalism's bitterest enemies. From the eighth century onward the words of the prophets have been preserved for us, and it is to these that we must now turn for further help in understanding man's quest for religious certainty in one God.

The first of the writing prophets was Amos. At least his message has been recorded for us. Whether he wrote it himself or whether it has been preserved by others is relatively unimportant for our consideration at this point. His message has been remembered. It must be admitted, however, that it was not received enthusiastically at the time of its delivery. Amos attended the great religious gathering at Bethel. Had one consulted the priests, they would have insisted that there was every indication of a thriving religion. The crowds were large, the ritual beautiful, the offerings large, and the temple and its precincts were of the finest materials. But Amos had the conviction that the outward evidences of material well-being covered up an inner corruption. The lives of men were not being challenged. Leadership had failed in its responsibility. The whole performance was shallow and insincere. Even worse was the fact that the religion of Israel had surrendered to Baalism. The name of Yahweh was still used, but religion as practiced was nothing but nature worship. The sole purpose of its acceptance by the people was to bring them material prosperity. Magic was in greater evidence than was worship.

All of this was recognized by Amos. In a voice heavy with sarcasm and strong in denunciation he condemned this false thinking (4:4-5). It was transgression, not worship. Gifts were made either in response to the demands of a mechanical enactment of the ritual or because of a desire to be recognized as a generous contributor to the Temple. This desire for publicity of one's acts of generosity had its counterpart in the time of Jesus and led him to denounce those who loved to pray standing on street corners. In each case the adulation of the crowd was the only reward sought by the supposed worshiper.

In the opening words of this same chapter Amos indicates that the very terminology of Baalism had invaded the courts of the Temple of Yahweh. The leaders strutted; but instead of referring to themselves as "pillars of the church," they used the expression "bulls of Bashan." The bull, as we have already noted, was one of the important symbols of Baalism. It was so used because of the great strength of the bull and because of its creative powers. It is to the wives of such leaders that Amos turns and addresses as the "cows of Bashan," not an altogether complimentary term but one surcharged with meaning derived from Baalism. Amos is the first recorded individual to recognize that Yahwism had indeed become Baalism. Its very terminology betrays that fact. The prophet's cry was a plea to recognize things for what they were.

Similarly, the prophet Hosea recognized the deception. His prophetic activity began in warfare against the Baal religion. His message has more allusions to this nature religion than any other biblical book. He goes somewhat further than Amos in his analysis. It is Hosea who first labeled the images of Baalism for what they were, the products of mechanics (8:1-6). A later religious thinker, whose name is unknown to us, edited the work of Hosea and inadvertently informed us that the problem persisted through the years. He put upon the lips of Hosea the words "For I will put away the names of the Baals from her mouth, and they shall no longer be invoked by their name" (2:17). Those words are a confession that in the later period the religion of Baal still had strong hold upon the nation. The images of Baal and of the mother goddess have been found in varying quantities from all periods of Hebrew history, and in no period is there a complete absence of these figurines, as indicated by archaeological investigation. Amos and Hosea were not completely successful in their fight against Baalism, but they did succeed in calling attention to the false thinking that had invaded the very buildings dedicated to the religion of Yahweh.

It is highly probable that the messages of Amos and Hosea were rejected by the people to whom they were delivered, but there seem to have been enough people who took those messages seriously that at least twice in later history the words of the prophets had tremendous influence. The first of those was the religious upsurge in reaction against the reigns of Manasseh (693-40/39) and Amon (640/39-38) which resulted in putting Josiah (638-8) upon the throne and prepared the way for the great reform of 621 B.C.

The second impact was made at the time of the Babylonian captivity (597-38). As Nebuchadnezzar's army captured Jerusalem and took captive many of its citizens, terror must have struck a fearful blow. Many were willing to concede that the Babylonian gods were more powerful than the God of the Hebrews and that therefore the Palestinians had been defeated. But there were others who remembered the warnings of prophets from an earlier day, prophets like Amos and Hosea. These men had warned that dependence upon international politics instead of trust in the ways of God would bring disaster. Now these warnings proved to be pertinent. It must have caused many to admit that the prophets had spoken with insight as well as conviction. Their words were worth gathering and remembering. Since other literature of their people was being gathered, it seemed appropriate to gather the words of the prophets. Whether there had been any collections made of the writings of the prophets before this time may never be known; but there is strong indication that during the bitter days of the Exile the words of the prophets, which formerly had been rejected or disregarded, were now cherished and preserved.

Let us turn again to a consideration of the first of these impacts of the teachings of the eighth-century prophets, the great reform under King Josiah. The immediate cause of the reform was the discovery of a scroll of law (II Kings 22, 23) during the repair of the Temple, and it is now generally admitted that this scroll of law is to be identified with the main part of the book of Deuteronomy. There is disagreement concerning the date of the writing of this law. Though suggested dates differ, it is well established that the document came as the result of the teachings of the eighth-century prophets and was produced somewhere between the close of the life of Isaiah and the discovery of the document in the Temple in the year 621 B.C. One of the major purposes of this scroll of law was to purge the religion of the Hebrews from all taint of Baalism and from nature worship. There were weaknesses in the reform, as we shall see later; but the reform inspired by this scroll of law did result in temporarily staying the forward surge of Baalism.

Throughout the book of Deuteronomy there is emphasized the idea of one God, who is to be worshiped at one shrine, which by implication is Jerusalem. It is admitted that centralization of power in Jerusalem had significant political implications as well as religious benefits. The emphasis upon one God and one shrine is highly significant in the history of religious development. It is an entirely new note, never uttered up to this time in all the stories that had been told of the Hebrew tribes and nation. This emphasis must have come as the result of the teachings of the prophets, who were the first to discover and to teach that there is but one God. It is necessary, then, for us to turn back to the messages of the eighth-century prophets and see the contribution that each made to man's understanding of the nature of God.

Perhaps never in the history of the Hebrews was there a century so filled with great religious pioneers as the eighth century B.C. This is not to say that it was the golden age of prophecy and the climax of religious discovery, and that from henceforth there was a decline both in prophecy and in religious advancement. The fact is that the great advances made by the Hebrews were after this period and not during it. The prophets of this period found no immediate responses to their challenges. It is likewise true that there were discoveries in religion made in later centuries that were as truly significant as the ones made by Amos, Hosea, Isaiah, and Micah; but the fact remains that there is no other period in Old Testament history when as many men of so noble stature appeared within a period of fifty years. And since all of them contributed so greatly to man's understanding of ethical monotheism, we may appreciate why the Hebrews and historians alike have glorified this period and have deprecated, or at least underestimated, the significance of discoveries made in later periods.

The first of these great religious leaders was Amos. We shall see later [4] how the mind of this man worked and what it was that led him to his great discoveries. We are concerned just now with the discovery and not the discoverer. At first glance it may seem illogical to separate a man from his message; but it is hoped that by examining first the succession of related religious discoveries, we may understand and appreciate the significance of these discoveries in the history of mankind. Later we shall examine the experiences in relation to the personalities of the prophets, and by examining them in succession we should have

[4] See Chapter Eleven, pp. 151 ff.

greater appreciation for the importance of personality in religion.

To Amos belongs the credit for the first clear-cut message that there is but one God and that the nature of that God is moral. There is a sternness about the message of this prophet that is all but repelling. Indeed, its very sternness led to his expulsion from the shrine at Bethel. As Amos looked upon the failure of religious and political leadership in the Northern Kingdom, he was impelled to stress five aspects of religion. First was the principle of monotheism. For Amos, Yahweh was the controller of all nations, and therefore there was no place in his thinking for other national deities (Amos 4:6-11). Second, he was convinced that the very nature of God was moral, and as such he had a right to demand moral conduct on the part of his creation (2:6 ff.; 5:10-13, 21-27). Third, he contradicted a popular teaching of his day, namely, that because Israel was a chosen nation, therefore a day of the Lord would bring happiness and triumph particularly over Israel's political enemies. Amos insisted that privilege implies responsibility, and that since Israel had had greater knowledge of the mind of God but had failed to live according to that knowledge, therefore the day of the Lord would be even more intolerable for Israel than for its neighbors (5:18-20). His fourth emphasis was a development of the third principle, and he stressed that sin must inevitably bring punishment.

There are those who feel that the message of Amos is almost exclusively condemnation. We must insist, however, that the apparent purpose of Amos' teaching is to call the nation to repentance, yet the message was delivered in the hope that some change would result (6:1 ff.).[5] He may have been pessimistic concerning the probable response of the nation, but he spoke in challenge and not despair. Finally, the prophet urged the necessity for sincerity in worship and condemned the substitution of elaborate but meaningless liturgy for moral living (4:4-5). His five principles revolved about the central fact of the moral nature of God. His message was stern, and it needed the corrective of the message of Hosea, but it became the foundation on which other teachers could build the fully developed structure of ethical monotheism.

[5] See p. 155 below.

The sternness of the message of Amos was balanced by the discovery of Hosea that God has a love and a concern for man. This, too, was a new concept in religion. Strangely enough, Hosea was unconsciously guided to this new idea by the very practices of the religion he fought so bitterly, the worship of Baal. Out of the love life of the gods, dramatized so sensationally by the devotees in the temples, it was believed that there came great benefits to man. The grain grew, animals multiplied, and olives ripened. It was but a step from the belief that the connubial life of the deities was necessary to the production of food for man to a belief that perhaps the deities did these things on behalf of man. Yet Baalism never seems to have arrived at that concept. Perhaps Hosea's concept developed by way of contrast. In any case Hosea is the first man of historical record to announce God's love for man. Indeed, he went beyond the simple avowal of divine love toward man and insisted that the love of God yearns for the answering love of man. There is emphasis upon the possibility of companionship, not mere servitude.

Unfortunately love has been looked upon as something weak and effeminate, but this is far from the concept of Hosea. He portrays strong and powerful love, not weak sentimentality. There is judgment as well as forgiveness in the message of Hosea. He is concerned that leaders and people alike have constantly violated the moral laws of God. He is not a preacher of a social gospel, for he is far more concerned that man is breaking the law of God and so offending him than that in the breaking of these laws other men are hurt. The judgment is from God and not an aroused public conscience. Another eight centuries had to pass until man came to understand that love for God must be reflected in man's love for his fellow.

Still another great thinker of the eighth century was the prophet Isaiah. It is generally recognized that chapter six records Isaiah's challenge to prophecy. We shall note that chapter again as we consider man's growth in worship, but it is needful here to consider the significance of the opening sentences. King Uzziah died in 739 B.C. It is altogether possible that Isaiah was in the Temple mourning his death. Jewish tradition tells us that Isaiah was cousin to the king, but it is a legend for which we have no historical proof. The death of the king must have caused much consternation among the people, for he had been a good ruler for thirty years.

Isaiah may have shared in the general apprehension concerning the future of the country in the hands of a new and untried leader. It was in this moment of anguish that the conviction came to him that God was king, that it mattered but little who was the earthly representative so long as the people recognized that God was their great ruler. Throughout his life Isaiah centered his message around this conviction of the majesty of God, and the suzerainty of the Deity was not confined to the lands of Israel and Judah. It compassed the earth. No ruler of nations could therefore thwart the purposes of God without inevitable catastrophe. To be sure, the seat and center of Yahweh's domain was in Jerusalem, but this does not indicate a contradiction in the thought of Isaiah. His insistence upon the inviolability of Jerusalem derived from his conviction that God controls the nations.

This concept of the majestic power of the Deity was another needful element in the construction of monotheism. It is an emphasis needed in the message of religion today. Far too much emphasis has been made in some quarters upon a blind, unthinking force of nature to the exclusion of the concept of the purposive and creative power of an ethical Deity.

There was danger in Isaiah's portrayal of God the king. It eventuated in the postexilic period in a picture of a God far removed from mundane affairs. He was completely transcendent, and the necessity for the mediation of priests and heavenly messengers was quickly invented by the ever-fertile mind of the professional religionists. All this was far from the mind of Isaiah. God was a great ruler and all-powerful, but God was also very near and deeply concerned about the welfare of mankind.

The religion of this period has been well summarized in the message of Micah, another stalwart of the eighth century:

> With what shall I come before the Lord,
> And bow myself before God most high?
> Shall I come before him with burnt-offerings,
> With calves a year old?
> Will the Lord be pleased with thousands of rams,

With myriads of streams of oil?
Shall I give my first-born for my transgression,
The fruit of my body for the sin of my soul?
You have been told, O man, what is good,
And what the Lord requires of you:
Only to do justice, and to love kindness,
And to walk humbly with your God?
(Mic. 6:6-8.)

For the people and many of their religious leaders there was still an insistence upon ceremonialism and the strict demands of mechanical rites. But the prophets insisted that the God of all people demands changed conduct and sincere service.

Eighth-century religion, as taught by the prophets and as practiced by the people, had one major hindrance to the complete evolvement of ethical monotheism; and that was the centrality of the nation in every major concept. The Hebrews believed that it was the nation with whom God had made the covenant. Success came to the nation in the form of material blessings from God only in so far as the nation followed divine mandate. Punishment was inflicted upon the nation and not individuals. The only punishment that came to the individual was that decreed by the social group in its attempt to purge itself of unrighteousness. The burden upon the individual was largely that of maintaining his position as an acceptable member of society. Blessings came to him or punishment came to him in common with all other members of the social group with whom the Deity had made agreement.

There had been indications of a break in this rigid pattern. As the prophets charged the leaders, political and religious, with dereliction of duty, it involved the principle of personal moral responsibility. But the discovery that each individual is personally responsible before God for his conduct had not yet been made. Many factors entered into the development of this tenet of religion. The principle is first clearly expressed by the prophets Jeremiah and Ezekiel.

Jeremiah began his work more than a hundred years after Isaiah had begun his. Many changes had come into the national scene. The Northern Kingdom had now disappeared. The Southern Kingdom had remained intact only by becoming a vassal state to Assyria. Now the Assyrian empire was declining in power; and a new power was developing, the Neo-Babylonian Empire, or the Chaldeans. Changes had come in the religious field. After the reigns of Manasseh and Amon there had been revolt, and Josiah had been placed upon the throne of Judah. The great reform had been set in motion, but personal political ambitions of Josiah had led to his death at the hands of Pharaoh-Necho. Faster and still faster the political scene changed. Judah was caught in the web of its own political machinations. It was evident to any keen observer that its days were numbered.

Jeremiah sensed that if religion was to be saved, then it had to be disentangled from nationalism. The nation had developed a philosophy that found its expression in the proverb

> The fathers eat sour grapes,
> And the children's teeth are set on edge.

It was expressed also in the Decalogue: "Punishing children for the sins of their fathers, to the third or fourth generation" (Exod. 20:5). Jeremiah insisted that each man was responsible for his own sin and that there was neither transfer of credit nor transfer of condemnation. Coupled with Jeremiah's declaration of individual moral responsibility was his announcement of God's willingness to forgive the penitent (Jer. 31:27-34; Deut. 5:9-10).

From the same period and surroundings there came two diametrically opposed movements: that of Jeremiah's toward individual responsibility and personal salvation, and that of the Deuteronomic reform which led toward legalism, institutionalism, and sacerdotalism. Jeremiah's distrust of the institution may have given urgency to his message of individualism, as has been pointed out.[6] Jeremiah's enthusiasm for his new discovery led him to an unfortunate underevaluation of the institution. That is ever the danger that faces the prophet. But it was the very institution he discountenanced that conserved and painstakingly taught his message. The prophets were restlessly impatient, looking for immediate reformation. The institution owed its very life to its discovery that patience is in-

[6] *Abingdon Bible Commentary* (New York and Nashville: Abingdon Press, 1929), p. 679.

dispensable to the teaching process, and teaching was one of its main reasons for existence. Jeremiah, too, was concerned about the wrong conception that people held of a "covenant" with God. Early in their history they had been inspired by a tradition of a covenant written upon stone. During Jeremiah's lifetime they were rejoicing in the discovery of a covenant written upon papyrus or parchment which they hailed as the "law of God." Jeremiah insisted that the only covenant worth while was that which was written upon the hearts of men, the hearts of individuals.

A contemporary of Jeremiah was another priest turned prophet, Ezekiel. While Jeremiah remained in Jerusalem, the young priest Ezekiel went into Babylonian captivity. There are strange similarities and contrasts involved in the lives of these two men. They were poles apart in their evaluation of the Temple as an institution. They were likewise in utter disagreement as to the place of communal worship in the life of the individual. Symbolism was an essential element in Ezekiel's organization of the religious community, but it was unnecessary in Jeremiah's scheme of life. There was complete agreement, however, in their asseveration of personal moral responsibility.

Since the major part of their lives was spent in completely different environments, there must have been differing contributing factors which helped them to arrive at their conviction concerning the moral life. Ezekiel undoubtedly served his fellow countrymen as a counselor and guide. There was no opportunity to offer burnt offerings and sacrifices as had been their custom in the homeland. The time had come again for religion to minister in new ways or cease to be. Men in exile discovered the value of private religious disciplines. They made the discovery that prayer was as meaningful in Babylon as in Palestine. The God of the Hebrews was not confined to Palestinian soil as they had formerly believed. Bitter as were the experiences of exile, yet religious knowledge was broadened through those experiences.

It was particularly necessary for the priest Ezekiel, if he was to minister to the needs of his countrymen, to find new emphases in the functions of religion. Like Jeremiah he arrived at the conviction that ethical religion must revolve about the individual in his relation to his God. Ezekiel was likewise persuaded that God would forgive the truly penitent transgressor. The clearest expression of forgiveness before New Testament times is given to us by this prophet (31:18, and so on). Perhaps Ezekiel knew that in the past the Temple as an institution had failed to minister to men, but during the Exile the institution made its atonement and lost its life in service to men. Ezekiel dreamed of a resurrected nation. He was so convinced that organized religion which gave itself in service to men could not die that he dared to write an ecclesiastical constitution for his theocratic utopia. But in writing his utopia he was more practical than the idealist Jeremiah, for he recognized that man is in constant need of guidance and encouragement to avail himself of the dynamic of religion.

Thus step by step and under the guidance of religious pioneers man has come from the place of belief in many gods to a belief in a Creator who is moral, who is concerned about his creation, who yearns for the love of men, and with whom there is forgiveness. Religion has ceased to be magical incantation by the shaman on behalf of the community, but it is now communion of the individual with his Creator, and the truly religious individual is concerned to bring his life into harmony with the moral laws of the Creator.

6

Religion Becomes Moral

Law Codes

RELIGION IS NOT NECESSARILY MORAL. A STUDY OF THE HISTORY of religions indicates that religion comes first to the place of placating the deities and only later, if indeed at all, thinks in terms of the religious necessity for moral conduct. The religion of the Hebrews according to the Bible was for many centuries without an understanding of the moral nature of the universe, the moral nature of its Creator, and consequently the religious necessity for moral conduct of man.

Man's first sense of moral responsibility was to the community in which he lived and not to his God. The reason for this was, as we have noted, that it was believed that the community as a whole was punished or blessed by the gods; and as a consequence society purged itself of wrongdoers simply as a means of self-defense. The final discovery that man is personally responsible before God for his conduct was the climax of a long journey in religious adventure.

how did "discover" e this?

One of the greatest sources of information on this particular adventure is the law of the Hebrews. Under the leadership of the great men of Israel the Hebrews came to discover religious and moral truths of the universe. It is true that the leaders were not always followed, nor did the people immediately respond to the moral challenge of their leaders, yet there is indication that the lawmakers of Israel gradually changed the law of the Hebrews so that it was in harmony with the moral teachings of the leaders. By arranging the various law codes of the Hebrew people in the chronological order of their writing, it is possible for us to reconstruct the growth in moral understanding that came to the Hebrews.

We should note that there was no distinction between civil and religious law in the Hebrew community. There was no separation between church and state. God was thought to be the head of the community; hence the law codes treated not only ecclesiastical regulations but also that which we today call civil law. Ecclesiastical law is often more concerned with the control of rites and ceremonies and the regulation of the religious institution and its leadership; civil law is primarily concerned with man's conduct as it affects life and property. It is in this latter area that we are most likely to discover the level to which moral understanding has come. We shall therefore examine carefully both phases of Hebrew law.

Moses has been recognized as the outstanding lawgiver of the Hebrews, but there were law codes in existence before his birth, and there were law codes enacted after his death. It became traditional among the Jews to refer to all codified law as the law of Moses, and this has led to the misunderstanding both by Jews and by Gentiles that Moses is the actual author of the law so designated. Yet we do not insist that Noah Webster originated all the words in the dictionary, nor indeed that he is even the compiler of the recent editions of Webster's Dictionary. We are grateful, therefore, for the discoveries of biblical scholarship which may prevent us from falling into that pitfall of false thinking, one author for all biblical law.

The question arises, then, by what means we are able to determine the various dates of Hebrew law, for naturally this must be done before we can arrange the law in chronological sequence. There are many clues. The first clue is that of history itself. We know from their own story something of the many environments under which the Hebrews lived. For many years the tribes wandered in the desert. Later they entered the "promised lands" and became agriculturists. Still later they conquered the large cities of Palestine, and many of the people became city dwellers. Different law is needed for city life than for desert or country life. Such differences in law may be recognized in the Bible.

Another clue is that of language. Hebrew language was used for many centuries before it became a dead language. During that time it changed considerably due to the regular rules that apply to all spoken languages. New words came into the vocabulary either as loan words from neighboring nations or because of the necessities of life. The American language has many rich additions because of words that have been picked up by men in military service stationed in foreign lands, particularly those lands in which English is spoken. Grammatical changes also affected Hebrew dialects and language.

If we should come across an essay which included quotations from Chaucer, Shakespeare, George Bernard Shaw, and Mark Twain, even though those quotations were not identified or designated by quotation marks, we should have no difficulty in recognizing differences in style; and perhaps we should even be able to identify the original writers or at least the period in history in which each portion was written. Similarly in Hebrew language we can recognize variations in style and the periods to which each style belongs. Unfortunately we are not able to assign writings to specific writers, and we must be content with designating various writings by means of a letter or other convenient symbol.

Still another valuable clue is called "internal evidence." If, for example, we picked up a scrap of newspaper from which the date had been torn and any identification which would indicate the date of publication and read a report on a speech by a president of the United States, there probably would be enough information there for us to identify the speaker and perhaps the approximate date on which the speech was made. If the President used the phrase "the forgotten man" and went on to talk of Pearl Harbor, General MacArthur conquering the Philippines and turning over authority to the civil government, but made no mention of the offer of the Japanese to surrender, then we could deduce that the President was Franklin D. Roosevelt and that the speech was made sometime after February 26 and before August 14, 1945. Similar deductions may be made from internal evidence in Hebrew literature, and this is particularly true of the legal writings. These are the chief clues; and though there are others, we need not at this time concern ourselves with them. Suffice it to say that a scholar is expected to have carefully checked evidence before submitting proposals for dating any portion of literature.

Law necessary for the regulation of tribes in the desert was quite different from the law needed when the Hebrews invaded the land of Palestine. The fact of the matter is that the oldest codes of law known to have been used by the Hebrews are codes that were already in existence in settled communities. They bear no evidence of having been appropriate for desert life. Just when the Hebrews became acquainted with these regulations is not altogether certain. There is clear evidence from archaeological investigation that some of the law codes, later adapted by the Hebrews to their own particular needs, were known in written form several hundred years before the Hebrews attained to national consciousness. In each case the law code is that suitable for a settled agricultural or urban society and was therefore probably accepted by the Hebrews after their entry into Canaan. There are also regulations which seem to have been preserved from the traditions of the desert. Those regulations were often preserved through the custom of the community rather than in a formal legislative code. Tribal organization and ethic persisted to a very late date. There was a tendency of the prophets to idealize tribal ethic and to denounce practices which had arisen in association with agricultural and urban societies. There was a resulting tension between prophet and people. There was a constant tension also between those who had power under tribal organization and those who advocated centralization of power under the monarchy. As the tensions between vested interests and reform groups continued, other groups entered the struggle with the final result that power was divided among many groups. Pleas have been made in recent times for recognition that democracy had its inception among the Hebrews, but it should be recognized that diffusion of power is not democracy; it is merely compromise of pressure groups. Democracy is not possible without recognition of the importance of the individual and his rights, and this came very late in the history of the Hebrew people.

One of the oldest codes in our Bible is the Primitive Code, Exod. 34:17-26. It bears evidence of having been edited and revised to meet changing religious convictions, but the general structure of the code indicates its appropriateness for the agricultural society into which the invading Hebrews were absorbed. It is a code of ten laws similar in many ways to the more familiar Decalogue in Exod. 20 and Deut. 5. We note that this Primitive Code is not only specifically prepared for an agricultural community, but it is entirely inappropriate for wandering tribes of the desert, except as they may have on a few occasions planted a crop. The feasts are all associated with planting, harvesting, and other phases of farm life. There is an indication that some, if not all, of these laws were in use by the Canaanites before the invasion of the Hebrew tribes. The laws were perhaps modified to fit the later religious convictions of the Hebrews. Since it is now believed by many scholars that there was more than one invasion of Palestine by tribal groups, the question at once arises, With which invasion and tribal confederation is this code to be associated? [1] For this we have no conclusive answer; but it is altogether possible that this code was adopted by the earlier invaders who became the forebears of the northern confederacy, later known as the kingdom of Israel. In any case it is clear that the code had its inception in an agricultural community and that it was modified to harmonize with the developing religious concepts of the Yahweh religion.

The second observation concerning this code is that its emphasis is entirely upon ritualistic demands and not upon the relationships of men in society. Careful attention is given to the correct preparation of the gifts to be brought to the Deity and under what circumstances these gifts are to be presented. There is an indication that the presentation of such gifts, particularly the first-born and first fruits, was an act of propitiation whereby the remainder was made safe for man's use after the Deity's claim to "first" fruits had been met. It is the level of fear and magic. It is completely alien to later religious conviction that gifts to God's work are first claims upon income, not because of fear but because the response of man's love to God's love demands it.

Another law code of early origin is the Covenant Code, Exod. 21–23, so named because of its association with the covenant on Mount Sinai. Like the Primitive Code it is more suitable to a settled agricultural community than it is to desert life. Domesticated animals have an unusually large amount of attention given to them in this group of regulations; and this can be due only to the fact that the code, wherever it may have been written, is designed as the basis of peaceful settlement of difficulties which may arise among farmers. In this particular case we have specific information concerning its history before it became a part of the Hebrew code of laws.

[1] Olmstead, *History of Palestine and Syria* (New York: Chas. Scribner's Sons, 1931), p. 195, n. 4.

In 1902 a French expedition to Susa, Persia, made some interesting discoveries including a great stele, or column, of black diorite. This column is almost eight feet high and varies in circumference from six feet at the bottom to five feet at the top. The top third of the face of the stele portrays Hammurabi, king of the Babylonians, standing in reverence before Shamash, the Babylonian god. The god is seated and is presenting to Hammurabi symbols of authority much like the symbols always seen in the hands of the Egyptian Pharaohs. The significance of the picture is that the king derives his authority, and perhaps his law, from his god. The remainder of the column, obverse and reverse, is covered with Babylonian writing. More than 3,600 lines of writing are to be seen on this monument. Translation reveals that this column was prepared at the orders of Hammurabi and is a list of Babylonian laws from nearly four thousand years ago. There are the regular long introductory and closing paragraphs devoted to glorification of the ruling monarch. The rest is law, probably based upon actual cases presented in the Babylonian city for adjudication. Law in those days seems to have been based largely upon precedent, and this placing of a list of solved cases on a public monument was done with the purpose of guiding future conduct and decisions in the country.

Evidence is now at hand which indicates that much of the law on this column had its inception not with the Babylonians but with the Sumerians, a non-Semitic people who inhabited the Mesopotamian valley before the Babylonian Empire was established. Careful comparison of the Hammurabi Code with the Covenant Code reveals some startling similarities. Not only are the same problems treated, but in many cases the phrasing of the sentences is similar. There are differences, too, and the differences are perhaps more significant than the similarities. Whoever was responsible for the introduction of the Covenant Code into Hebrew literature not only knew legislation of at least one foreign country but was highly selective in his borrowing. Further, careful adaptation is made to the special needs of the Hebrew community. For example, in the Hammurabi Code provision is made for the release of the slave at the end of three years of service. In the Covenant Code release is to be made in the seventh year. This may be due to the lower value of labor in Palestine, and perhaps there is an attempt to create a Sabbath of the years to correspond to the Sabbath of the week. The differences indicate that morals are beginning to enter into the thinking of men. There are real attempts here to see that justice between men is possible regardless of the economic condition of plaintiff or defendant.

The Ten Commandments (Exod. 20:1-17; Deut. 5:6-21) are so well known to us that it is needful only to note that in them we have a bringing together of regulations concerning man's relation to his God and man's conduct toward his fellow man. The ethic of the Ten Commandments, just as of any other set of religious laws in those days, applied only within the tribal relationships.[2] Beyond that it was permissible to plunder, steal, and kill. Only after long experience did men discover that these laws are of fundamental significance and are as valid in international relations as within one's own nation. Indeed, there is some question whether we have learned that lesson yet, for there are those who would teach that moral conduct shall be one thing for men as individuals, but when they move as a nation, another ethical code must be substituted.[3]

In spite of the fact that men had now accepted for themselves a moral code, they had no thought that God was a moral being. An appallingly high percentage of the religious people in the world today are in the same stage of religious immaturity. For them the divine Power is simply power without moral restraint. It is that men believed in not an immoral god but an amoral one. Such a picture is given in I Kings 22:2 ff. Ahab, king of Israel, sought political alliance with the southern tribes of Judah for the purpose of regaining from the nation Syria a city known as Ramoth in Gilead. Jehoshaphat, king of Judah, was willing to enter into the alliance if it could be demonstrated that this was in accordance with the will of God; for no king went into battle in those days except with the knowledge that his god was on his side. Four hundred prophets were consulted, and they were unanimous that the campaign should proceed. But Jehoshaphat wanted to hear from one other prophet,

[2] Rowley, *op. cit.*, pp. 157 ff.

[3] Cf. Louis Wallis, *The Bible and Modern Belief* (Durham, N. C.: Duke University Press, 1949) ; and Fred V. Winnett, *The Mosaic Tradition* (Toronto: University of Toronto Press. 1949).

Micaiah, the son of Imlah. Ahab of Israel consented grudgingly, for apparently Micaiah's former prophecies had not fitted into the king's plans. Warned of the unanimous message of the four hundred, Micaiah nevertheless insisted that he would speak his conviction, not merely endorse royal desires. Strangely enough, when he did speak to King Ahab, his words were in precise agreement with the others. But something in the tone of his voice or the expression on his face made the king suspicious. It was then that Micaiah voiced the message he felt impelled to deliver. He portrayed the Deity sending a lying spirit among the other prophets and so perverting their messages in order that King Ahab's life should be destroyed in battle. It is a naïve tale and one that raises many questions. Among them we may well wonder at the intelligence of a Deity who would permit one lone prophet to upset a plan carefully arranged in the councils of heaven. This would make Micaiah more powerful than God. More important is the consideration as to the moral nature of a Deity who would enter into such an arrangement. The weakness, of course, was with man's lack of understanding of the nature of God. The four hundred have been labeled false prophets, but in the light of later knowledge Micaiah's description of the nature of God is far from correct.

In rapid succession there came the great prophets of the eighth century B.C., who completely changed the patterns of religious thought. Perhaps the most outstanding influence of their work upon the literature of Israel was on the code of law found in the Temple of Jerusalem in 621 B.C. The content of that law code and the circumstances under which it was found all point to the probability that it was written by men who had been inspired by the messages of the eighth-century prophets. This document became important for several reasons. It was the immediate cause of the reform under King Josiah in which the religion of Yahweh was centralized in Jerusalem and the religion of Baal was officially destroyed. It is the only portion of that collection of Hebrew law known as Torah which gives any place to the love of God. The law was read to the people, and they accepted it as the law of the community. With the people's acceptance of the idea that this law was identical with the will of God for them, there developed the concept of "scripture." It was around this nucleus of law that other law was gathered, and eventually it became the core around which the whole Old Testament was collected. This document was not a formal code enacted by a legislature. Rather it was an ideal for which the nation strove. It had its faults as well as its virtues, concession to Josiah's political ambitions being among them. The chief difficulty lay in the attempt to confine religion to a written document, however noble that document may have been. It was this that led to later legalism and Pharisaism. Yet in spite of these faults the discovery of this law in the Temple introduced into Hebrew life a far higher moral code than it had ever known before.

Justice for all regardless of one's social standing was made the ideal of the Hebrew community through this new law. The Sabbath is made to serve man and not man the Sabbath. Woman was now looked upon as something more than chattel. Throughout the law, which has been preserved in the book of Deuteronomy, there was constant effort to protect the religion of the Hebrews from contamination by contact with other religions. There was a closer identification of the religion of Yahweh and social justice than there had ever been before. The poor man and his family were given special consideration. It is from Deuteronomy that the Jews have drawn their great statement of religious belief. It was from this same book, too, that Jesus drew his description of the heart of religion: "The Lord is our God, the LORD alone; so you must love the Lord your God with all your mind and all your heart and all your strength" (Deut. 6:4-5).

In less than twenty-five years after the adoption of this law by the Hebrews, the first group of the inhabitants of Jerusalem had gone into Babylonian captivity; and eleven years later Jerusalem was destroyed, and the nation ceased to exist as a political entity. Some of the people were quick to associate their change in political fortune with this adoption of Yahweh's law and religion. They remembered that the prophetess Huldah had promised that because King Josiah had accepted the responsibility for the national adoption of this newly found law and had repented on behalf of the nation, he would live a long and happy life and die a peaceful death. They assumed, also, that prosperity would come to the nation Israel. Neither happened, and they assumed that it would have been better for them to have remained faithful to the Queen of Heaven, a title by which the wife of Baal was known (Jer. 44:25 ff.). They failed to see that Josiah's death came in a battle with the Egyptians in which he was seeking to protect his own political ambitions.

As the Hebrew people went into political slavery in Babylon, they took with them this law; and it had a great influence upon their thinking during that particular phase of their national experience. Around this law as a nucleus, as we have noted, other law was gathered. Three distinct bodies of law may be recognized. First, there was the law of Ezekiel. There is some disagreement as to whether or not Ezekiel lived in the sixth century or was responsible for chapters forty to forty-eight in the book of Ezekiel. Yet it would seem that the message of Ezekiel is incomplete without this picture of utopia given in the closing chapters of his book. They are in accord with the spirit of the prophet and in any case were produced after the law of Deuteronomy.

Ezekiel's utopia is a curious mixture of wishful thinking and practical suggestions for social justice and religious perfection. God is at the center of the new Jerusalem. The very name of the city is to be changed from Jerusalem to *Jehushama,* which means "God is there." Plans for the construction of the temple are given in minute detail, and it is possible to draw blueprints of the floor plans from his description. Every effort is made to guard the holiness of this sacred place. Special cubicles are provided in which the priest shall robe, leaving all street clothes and worldly contact behind as he goes on into the temple area. The uncircumcised are strictly barred from this sacred area. Marriage of the priests is carefully regulated so as to ensure the purity of the priesthood. Wine is forbidden in the temple ceremonies, possibly in an attempt to avoid any semblance of the rites of the Baal religion.

Priests are to be the judges, and an impartiality of judgment is preserved by decreeing that such priests shall have lifetime appointment (they are not subject to re-election); they shall have homes, clothing, and food provided for them (guaranteed income); and they shall own no property (and so cannot be bribed) . There is to be a fixed system of weights and measures —a policy pleaded for by eighth-century prophets.

It is in the social and political scene that wishful thinking is so prominent. The land is to be restored to the full extent of the old Davidic empire; and all the tribes will have their allotted portions, not, however, their old territories. Great fertility is to abound, and there is to be a complete disregard of topography, It is assumed that there will be equal fertility in mountain and valley, and that even the coast line will be changed so that each tribe shall have an equal amount of land, "except that a double portion shall go to Joseph" (47:13) . An interesting picture is that of the river which is to flow beneath the temple. Apparently it flows in two directions, for each tribal unit is to have the benefits of this stream. Along the banks of the river trees will grow which shall always be in fruit and whose leaves shall have medicinal properties. The stream which flows south will purify the Dead Sea, but the industries on the banks of the Dead Sea which have depended upon impurities in the water shall not be disturbed. Yet there is practicality, too, about this section of law. Taxes shall be fixed and likewise the assessments for the temple. Property rights are guaranteed, and neither the temple nor the political leaders shall be able to take property from any man. Royal enclosures are likewise fixed for perpetuity. These provisions are to give stability to the community and to protect the rights of the more unfortunate members of society who seem ever in danger of losing what few possessions they have. This code of law clearly recognizes that it is the function of religion to help men live together in harmony and peace.

The second body of law which bears the imprint of Deuteronomic influence is the Holiness Code, Lev. 17–26. This, too, came into being, at least in its present form, during the days of the Exile. There is a strong priestly emphasis throughout this law code, with a stress upon an almost mechanical aspect of holiness. To touch a holy or an unclean thing made the person unclean. Holiness and physical purity are interchangeable terms in this body of law, and one searches in vain for a spiritual aspect of holiness. Yet these laws have served humanity well. We still observe in many churches and states the laws on "degrees of marriage" (18:6-18) . Justice in the payment of wages

(19:13), charity instead of spite in lawsuits (19:15), prohibition of talebearing (19:16), are all considered a responsibility of man in his covenant relation with God.

It is from this same code that Jesus drew his statement concerning the second great law of religion: "You must love your fellow as one of your own" (19:18). The law of justice has now become a definite part of the law of the community. It has sometimes been called the law of retaliation or law of revenge. This is a false description, for the emphasis is not upon taking life in revenge for another life but rather that only one life shall be forfeited in penalty for taking another's.[4] This was severe restriction upon the old law of blood revenge.

Though still in exile, the Jews looked forward to a day of restoration. In anticipation of that day they formulated laws that would make their community one of justice based upon their understanding of the laws of God. During the Exile and in the days immediately following there was great literary activity on the part of a group of individuals who have been labeled loosely "the priestly school." These are the men who were responsible for preserving the various documents which now appear in our Old Testament, who edited the writings of the prophets in the light of new developments and experiences of the nation, who interwove their interpretation of history into the already existing stories of the nation, and who formulated the law now known as the Priestly Code. Most of this law appears in the Books of Law, Genesis through Deuteronomy. But its influence is strong also in the historical books, Joshua to Kings, and in the books I and II Chronicles and Ezra-Nehemiah. It is doubtful if a separate priestly version of Hebrew history ever circulated independently; but since the responsibility for law rested with the priests, there must have been various codifications of law in circulation.[5]

The priests took their responsibility seriously; and from the priestly law which has been preserved in our Bible, it is evident that the social conditions of men were a major consideration of the priests. It is unfortunate that we have assumed that priests

[4] W. G. Williams, *Books of the Law* (New York and Nashville: Abingdon Press, 1945), pp. 101-2.

[5] L. B. Longacre, *The Old Testament: Its Form and Purpose* (New York and Nashville: Abingdon Press, 1945), pp. 58-80, for an opposing view.

were primarily concerned for their own welfare and for the maintenance of the institution which gave them sustenance. It is essential that we recognize that the bitter denunciation of the prophets against the priests were directed not at the office of the priest but against those priests who had failed to live up to the responsibilities in their functions as teachers and guides of the people. In the postexilic period there was an overemphasis upon institutionalism and an overglorification of the office of priesthood, but nevertheless the priests served God and the people well. Priestly law, scattered throughout the Old Testament, has become basic to much of the common law and to the formal legislation of Western civilization. This is not to say that the priests devised all the law now designated Priestly Code, for much of it had come from far-distant periods in history. It is the skillful blending of ancient and less ancient that makes it so difficult to discover what has actually come from the pen of the priests. Their task was one of editing, revising where necessary, and of creating new law when that became essential to the changing conditions under which men lived. That their task was done well is indicated by the fact that this law became the first and most sacred part of Hebrew scripture, Torah.

Except as prophetic religion is interpreted in terms of day by day living, put into rules that regulate daily life, the great goals remain visionary and dreams are barren. The principles may be sound; but only as application is made, do ideals become reality. This is the function of religious law. It brings the dreams of the prophet to earth. The tragedy is that so often men take the rules which the priest has formulated from the principles of the prophet and, instead of using them as the priest intended them to be used as a floor under one's endeavors, conceive them to be the top ceiling of life's conduct. Then religion becomes legalistic.

Other influences brought in high standards of conduct and formulations of patterns of living which are noteworthy. Among them were the writings known as "wisdom literature," such books as Job, Ecclesiastes, and so on. It has been recognized that this literature gave consideration to philosophical problems, but little recognition has been made of the high moral content of many of these writings. Job 31, called the "code of a gentleman" by Robert H. Pfeiffer,[6] is perhaps the highest standard of moral conduct to be found in Old Testament writings. The opening verse—"I imposed a rule on my eyes; How, then, could I give heed to a virgin"—reminds us of the principle of Jesus that it is inner conviction rather than outward conduct that is important. The remainder of the chapter is a series of vows by Job that he has met the demands of high religion; that he has been concerned for the welfare of neighbors, employees, and indigent members of society; and that he has been faithful to the monotheistic concepts of Judaism. Here is the clearest expression of the religion of inner conviction, but inner conviction that manifests itself at least in part through outward conduct.

The Hebrew tribes began at the place of little relationship between the laws of religious regulation and the law of the civil community. Regulation of religious acts was largely governed by crude concepts of Deity. As they discovered the moral nature of the universe and its Creator, they began to apply this knowledge to themselves and to their community. With the insistence of the prophets that religion was a way of life, religious leaders began to think more clearly in terms of the application of religious principles to the world in which men lived. Social justice came to be at the heart and center of religious teaching and conduct. Until men had made this great step forward in their religious thinking, it was not possible for them to be ready for the message of Jesus as expressed in his law of love, the Golden Rule, and the Beatitudes. Prophets and priests prepared the "way of the Lord."

[6] *Introduction to the Old Testament* (Rev. ed., New York: Harper & Bros., 1948), p. 691.

7

From Magic to Worship

———◆———

MAGIC AND WORSHIP HAVE LONG BEEN ASSOCIATED. IN THE
earliest days of man little effort was made to distinguish between
the two. In modern times there are still those who continue
to confuse them. Definitions in terms of function will serve to
help us differentiate the one from the other. Magic, as related
to religious practices, consists of a knowledge of the right
techniques whereby supernatural powers may be brought under
man's control. Worship is homage paid to a divine power, and
in its highest expression man seeks to bring his life into
harmony with the laws of that divine power. Magic is man
centered and is essentially selfish. Worship is God centered
and is the spirit that cries, "Nevertheless not my will, but
thine, be done" (Luke 22:42 K.J.V.).

Any man who serves as the pastor of a church will soon discover that there is too close an association of magic and religion
in the minds of many people today. For example, there still
seems to be conviction that one's name properly inscribed upon
the records of some church, a baptism conducted in the proper
manner, or a properly phrased burial ritual correctly read will
guarantee salvation and reserved space in the mansions of the
blessed. Such gross misunderstanding of the function of worship
has led to suspicion in the minds of nonbelievers and has prevented the faithful from deriving from worship and religion the
strength they have to offer.

Some histories of religion indicate that all religion had its
inception in fear. Whatever may have been the first cause, it
must be confessed that fear has had an important part in
shaping the concepts of religion. Fear has been largely responsible for the magical aspects of religion. It is evidenced in the
conduct of the man in the jungle today. As he travels quickly

over the jungle trail, he may stumble over a stone in his path. Instead of removing that stone to make a smoother path for his return journey, he is much more likely to stop, place a protection about the stone, and pray, "O God, please do not trip me the next time I pass." He may bring offerings in order to assuage the anger of the god who so quickly hindered his journey. We may smile, but this man is at the stage of religious development at which we first find man as our Bible story opens.

Only a few remnants of the Stone Age of man remain clear in the biblical record. In Exod. 20:24 we have an indication that the first altars of man were made of earth. Nothing of these remains to be discovered by the archaeologist. In 20:25-26 we have regulations concerning altars of stone, stones untouched by man's tools. It is possible that such prohibition comes from the period when man believed the god to be resident in the stone, and to cut the stone would result in physical hurt to the god. The name "Bethel" seems first to have been used of stones erected as altars and only later applied to the "house of God." The name "Bethel" was a personal one and was used by the Hebrews and the Phoenicians alike in this significance.

The rite of circumcision is an old one, and the earliest Old Testament reference to this rite is clearly in Stone Age terms. Exod. 4:25 indicates that the first tools to be used in this ceremony were flint knives, a practice continued by Orthodox Jews of Europe until comparatively recent times. With which tribe or people circumcision originated, we do not know. The practice was widespread among many Semitic groups and the Egyptians. Its early significance seems to have been the sacrificial substitution of part of an organ for its whole or even for the whole person. The redemption of the whole by a substitution of a part is well-recognized magical procedure.

There is little wonder that so much magic intrudes upon the Bible record. From early until late the Hebrew people were virtually a wandering people and constantly found themselves among people who accepted magic as part of religion. For only small portions of their history were they settled in their homeland, and then so much of the time they were under the cultural and sometimes political domination of surrounding nations. Let us examine the magical practices of these neighboring nations, beginning with the Egyptians, whose influence is strong throughout Hebrew history.

An examination of Egyptian culture will reveal points at which magic has played a significant part. The art of the Egyptians reflects magical fear. It will be noticed that pictures inscribed or painted on walls of ancient tombs are incomplete. Whether the figure is that of man, bird, beast, or reptile, the figure is drawn in two parts with a slight break between the halves. There is purpose in this, for the Egyptians believed that if they should complete the figure, they would have created something which during the dark watches of the night might descend from the wall and do harm to man. I have seen a number of tombs in which the eye of the god has been gouged in order that he should not see the robbers at work.

The magical use of the name is another aspect known through Egyptian practices, ancient and modern. John A. Wilson, Egyptologist at the University of Chicago, found himself in the company of an Egyptian guide one time[1] who was most insistent, when he learned that Wilson could read the hieroglyphs, that the professor should tell him the names of the gods portrayed on the walls of the tomb. The guide's reason was not that he wished to be a better guide but that he should be prepared religiously. He stated it quite simply, "If I pronounce their names before they see me, I shall have power over them!" Literally, in that land there is power in the name. It is this same pattern of thinking that gives significance to the words of the Revelation that the faithful shall have a new name written upon stone, a name known to no one except the possessor and his God (2:17; 19:12; 22:4). Thus the possessor of the new name can no longer be controlled by Satan nor in the power of any man or evil force. The same type of thinking is to be found in the Koran. Allah is said to have one hundred names, but only ninety-nine of them are known to man. The one hundredth is known only to Allah. This is to insure that Allah shall remain free from all magical control. Classical and Near-Eastern mythology abounds in stories of trickery in celestial regions as the gods sought to discover the secret names of other gods in order to gain power over them.

[1] See my article in *The Iliff Review*, Winter, 1952, pp. 35-36.

A third area in which magic played a significant part in Egyptian thinking is in connection with burial practices. When Nanupkau (ca. 2500 B.C.) was making plans for himself and his wife, Hemetrezet, for their life in eternity, he planned carefully. Apparently Nanupkau had fared well in this life and was determined that he should continue to live happily in the life beyond this one. He believed that if the priest should intone the correct ritual over his body and the things buried with him then everything so buried would be transported with him into eternal bliss. He accordingly had copies carved in limestone of all the possessions he held important. The resulting models are exceedingly important for our studies in history and sociological conditions of 4,500 years ago.[2] All his servants and slaves are shown busy with their daily chores, and the tools necessary for their daily tasks are there. But Nanupkau knew that there were sometimes accidents in the tomb, and such models could be broken, thus making impossible their use for magical transportation to eternity. Of course he wanted to make sure that his wife would be awaiting his arrival; and whereas he had one copy made of each of his servants, he had two copies made of himself and his wife. Then he had two extra copies made of himself.

Somewhat later than this period the Egyptians began to bury their dead in coffins. Again magic was used to great advantage. When Ipi-Haishutep was buried, he made sure that he would be able to enter or leave his last resting place at will; for there is a door of magic drawn on his coffin for the convenience of his "ka," or spirit. He took advantage of another device. The magical eyes of Osiris are painted opposite the deceased's head so that without leaving his coffin he may still observe things on the outside.[3]

Many copies of the ancient Book of the Dead have been recovered and are to be seen in our museums.[4] The Egyptians believed it was essential that they be buried by the use of the right ritual. Accordingly they had made their own personal copy of the ritual with their names properly spelled and in-

[2] These statuettes may be seen at the Oriental Institute Museum of the University of Chicago, Egyptian Hall, Group K20, 10618-45.

[3] Oriental Institute Museum, Egyptian Hall, Group K17, No. 12072.

[4] Excellent copies are on display in the Egyptian Alcove at the Field Museum of Natural History, Chicago, Ill.

serted at the correct places. This was done to ensure that the priest would read the correct ritual. The poor man could not afford to buy the necessary ritual, so he merely took magic one step further. He had rolls carved of wood or stone, then wrapped a few layers of papyrus on the outside, and this was substituted for the more expensive complete copy. The Egyptians not only believed in magic, but they took every advantage that it offered them.

After leaving the land of Egypt, the Hebrews wandered in the desert for many years, then came into the land of Palestine. Upon their arrival they discovered that the Canaanites were in possession not only of the land but of a large amount of religious magic also. In addition to the practices which were parallel to those of surrounding nations, the Canaanites made an extensive practice of human sacrifice. In an earlier day Abraham had come into contact with this same people and their practices.

The familiar story of Abraham and Isaac needs re-examination in the light of our present knowledge of practices in Canaan. The story is significant not because of the offered sacrifice of Isaac but because the sacrifice was not offered. Abraham, in seeking to offer Isaac, was conforming to the accepted pattern of religious practice in which the first-born was regularly sacrificed to the Deity. We dare not underestimate the anguish of Abraham, though we have ignored Sarah's grief; but in our attempts to appreciate the faith of Abraham we have overlooked the great advance that he made over his contemporaries. He was ready to submit to precedent and offer Isaac, but suddenly the conviction came to him that God does not desire human sacrifice. Here is a break with an old established pattern. Abraham was the first to make the break, and we should honor him for having the courage of his conviction. To break with old precedents is not an easy thing to do. Human sacrifice, however, was not entirely abandoned either by the Canaanites or by the descendants of Abraham. In times of emergency men reverted to the old pattern.

In the period of the Judges, Jephthah was in conflict with the Ammonites. When war was inevitable, Jephthah made a vow to sacrifice whoever came through the door of his house upon his return with victory (Judg. 11:29-40). The King James

Version has translated this, "Whatsoever cometh forth of the doors of my house"; but "whatsoevers" do not go through doors. The Hebrew definitely indicates that the vow involved human sacrifice. Jephthah undoubtedly expected that he would be greeted by some slave or servant, but instead his daughter was the first to pass through the door to greet him. His grief was great, but neither he nor his daughter expected that the vow should be broken.

In times of national calamity it was not unusual for human sacrifice to be offered on behalf of the community. The King of Moab (II Kings 3:26-27) was unable to overcome the Edomites; and as the battle turned fiercely against him, he took his oldest son and offered him "as a burnt-offering upon the wall." Again the magic of human sacrifice had been appealed to.

It was because human sacrifice had been so prevalent that Micah's cry is so significant:

> With what shall I come before the Lord,
> And bow myself before God most high?
> Shall I come before him with burnt-offerings,
> With calves a year old?
> Will the Lord be pleased with thousands of rams,
> With myriads of streams of oil?
> Shall I give my first-born for my transgression,
> The fruit of my body for the sin of my soul?
> (6:6-7).

These penetrating questions lose much of their significance except as seen against the background of a society thoroughly conversant with the ways of human sacrifice.

Even in the late period of Hebrew history there is evidence that human sacrifice was still practiced. Foundation deposits and cornerstones have been found which give evidence that the original deposits made in cornerstones were those of human sacrifice. Usually the offering was that of a small child, the theory apparently being that when life left the body of the victim, it entered the building to give it life and strength. Photographs, newspaper clippings, and lists of subscribers to the building fund are just as effective and probably more informative for the future generations who shall uncover modern buildings. Further testimony to the late practice of human sacrifice is found in Lev. 27:28-29, where exemption from the vow to make such sacrifice is prohibited. This law is perhaps of great antiquity, but in its present form it was part of Hebrew legislation of the postexilic period and implies that the principle was at least tacitly approved at the late date.

The eighth-century prophets were most vehement in their disapproval of Canaanite magical practices. Amos (4:4-5; 8:4 ff.) and Hosea (13:2) have the clearest denunciation of these practices which by this time had come to be a part of the religion of Baal. As these same practices began to invade the Temple of Yahweh, particularly the shrine at Bethel, these prophets were quick to see that this sounded the death knell of ethical religion.

Strong influence from Babylonian magical practices was beginning to be felt. For political reasons King Ahaz permitted the symbolism of the Assyrian religion to be placed in the Temple at Jerusalem. An Assyrian altar fashioned after the pattern of the one at Damascus displaced the altar of Yahweh in the place of honor; but Ahaz protected himself by reserving for his own ceremonials the altar of Yahweh, which "shall be for me to inquire by" (II Kings 16:7-15).[5] A century later it became Josiah's task to clean out Assyro-Babylonian sun worship from the very roof of the Temple of Yahweh. In Babylonia the Hebrews again felt the pressure of Babylonian magical practices. It was Ezekiel this time who cried out against their acceptance. Some of the Hebrew women (Ezek. 13:17-23) had even taken up the practice of hunting for men's lives by magical incantations, the Babylonian equivalent of witchcraft.

The many provisions in Hebrew law which seek to guard against the intrusion of such practices, and the violence with which the prophets fought against these ideas, are testimony to the fact that the threat was real. But the prophets did more than denounce foreign and domestic magical practices; they sought to bring the people to higher concepts of worship. Perhaps the most outstanding description of an experience of worship is that of Isaiah at the time of his challenge to a prophetic career (Isa. 6:1-13).

The experience goes through the successive steps usually associated with private or corporate worship: a sense of personal

[5] See the discussion by Olmstead, *op. cit.*, p. 452.

need, an awareness of the presence of God, consciousness of one's sins or failures, forgiveness from God as confession is made, meditation which culminates in challenge from God, and the response of the individual to God's challenge. Elsewhere in his message Isaiah insists that such an experience is true worship and that God desires this rather than "fasting and festival" and the observance of great ceremonies (1:10-17).

A century later than Isaiah there appeared two men in rapid succession whose messages were important to the full development of Isaiah's concept of worship. Though this experience of Isaiah's was intensely personal, he did not discover that a sense of personal moral responsibility to God is a fundamental requirement of a satisfying worship experience. The messages of Jeremiah and Ezekiel were in agreement that religion is essentially a personal accomplishment and one of personal relationship to the Deity. Yet despite their complete agreement concerning the essential nature of worship, Jeremiah and Ezekiel were diametrically opposed in their consideration of the techniques of worship. Jeremiah seems to have been an idealist, and he dreamed of a day when men would have no need of the outward aids of religion, for out of the quiet of his own heart each man would be able to commune with his God. There would be no need of temple, of symbols, or of priests. His was the position of the quietist. He thoroughly denounced the folly of idolatry:

> "For the cults of the people are vanity—
> They are but a timber which one cuts from the forest,
> Which the carpenter's hands have wrought with the ax.
> Men deck it with silver and gold,
> Fasten it with hammer and nails,
> And set it up, so that it cannot move.
> They stand like scarecrows in a garden of cucumbers,
>   and cannot speak;
> They have to be carried, for they cannot walk.
> Be not afraid of them! for they cannot do harm,
> And also to do good is not in their power."
>   (Jer. 10:3-5.)

It may have been such use of physical aids to worship that led Jeremiah thoroughly to distrust man's ability to do anything but use symbols as idols. He knew that habits in religion become firmly fixed and are hard to eradicate even though man should have progressed to higher levels of thought. He cried out against "vain superstitions, which are good for nothing" and said quite frankly, "Our fathers inherited nought but lies" (16:19). Jeremiah seems to have accepted the Deuteronomic reform under Josiah and perhaps felt with others that now everything that was alien to the religion of Yahweh would be wiped out, and men would be led by the new law to the sense of moral responsibility that he himself felt. But not for long. Soon he denounced the new reform, hurling out his denunciation in no uncertain terms:

> How can you say, "We are wise,
> And the law of the Lord is with us?"
> When lo, the lying pen of the scribes
> Has turned it into a lie!
>
> (8:8.)

He lost all faith in institutional religion and saw that the solution to man's problems lay not in organization, in elaborateness of ceremonial, nor in the public approval of an idealistic code, but rather in the changed heart of each individual. The heart of his message is right here (cf. 31:31-34). The code upon stone had failed; so likewise had the new one discovered in the Temple and hailed so enthusiastically by the people. The great need of man was to have the law of God inscribed upon his heart—personal moral responsibility before God.

Overlapping in time with Jeremiah was Ezekiel. He began his work as a prophet shortly after the first group of captives had been transported to Babylonia. Ezekiel had gone with them. He must have known of the work of Jeremiah and may have been influenced by him. There is much similarity in their messages, but there are vital differences. Ezekiel appears to have been much more practical in his approach to the problems of men. He understood that the nature of many men is such that they need all the help that the externals of religion can give. In a modern world he would be called "high church," but to transport men from one civilization to another in a different hemisphere and at a distance of so many centuries is a dangerous thing to do. Ezekiel was answering the immediate needs

100

of his own day; and if we are tempted to accuse him of devotion to a priestly system, we must ever remind ourselves that it was this same Ezekiel who recognized that only a receptive heart could have the law of God inscribed upon it. It was this same Ezekiel who has been credited with being the father of the synagogue. Whether this be true or not, it is certain that Ezekiel saw a change from a temple-centered religion in Jerusalem to one that had little form but was the informal gathering of friends to share remembered words of the religious leaders and to breathe together a prayer for strength and deliverance. We cannot forget that it was from the Exile that there returned a remnant with a conviction that the leadership of Israel lay in its religious mission and message and not in any political or economic grandeur. There can be little doubt that Ezekiel, together with other religious leaders, helped to foster that great conviction. Perhaps it was his clear understanding of the help that organized religion could be that made him give the Temple and the priesthood so large a place in his teachings. But above and beyond all else was his deep understanding of the human heart and its need to be at peace with its God. The word "repent" rings out clearly again and again, and with it the clearcut teaching that God is ready and willing to forgive the truly penitent individual:

"Cast away from you all the transgressions which you have committed against me; and get yourselves a new heart and a new spirit. Why should you die, O house of Israel? For I have no pleasure in the death of anyone who dies," is the oracle of the Lord God. "Turn, then, and live!" (18:31-32.)

The function of priest as well as prophet in the mind of Ezekiel was to bring men to the place of repentance. When they came to this place, it was the function of organized religion to help man make his confession and bring to him the word of forgiveness. That normally is the work of the priest, and this Ezekiel clearly recognized. This insight of Ezekiel's that the great contribution of religion is to enable men to evaluate their conduct in the light of high standards is one of the noblest that the Hebrew prophets have given to mankind.

It would be unfortunate, however, to feel impelled to choose between the positions of Jeremiah and Ezekiel. The world of religious thinkers is still trying to do just that. And we have split the field of religion into two opposing camps: those who believe in little or no liturgy and those who rely quite heavily upon ritual and insist that others shall do likewise. Jeremiah and Ezekiel differed so extremely because of their different environments, but perhaps more because of their different psychological characteristics. So long as men are psychologically different, it would seem foolish to seek to force them into the same religious mold. We have taken this thing to the absurd length of insisting, at least in practice, that men shall fit one precise pattern to belong to this denomination, or if they belong to another pattern, they must of necessity join that other denomination. Until we recognize that within one church body we can care for men of varied tastes and psychological structures, it is useless for us to think in terms of uniting the various bodies of Christendom under the one banner of Christ.

Examination of the messages of the various prophets clearly indicates that they differed considerably concerning the matter of the use of ceremonies and liturgy. But there is no disagreement in their insistence that the sincerity of the worshiper is the basic ingredient in true worship. We may well consider what might be the reactions of an ancient prophet if he could but observe a modern church service with the keen analysis with which Amos observed the worship at Bethel. He might wonder as he observed the minister strut upon the platform, seeking throughout the service to call attention to himself rather than the God whom presumably the people have gathered to worship. He might wonder at the "entertainment" by the choir, who insist upon being seated so that "they may be seen of men," draped across the front of the auditorium and conducted in good concert-hall style.

He would be puzzled during the pastoral prayer to see the maneuvers of the choir in preparation for the anthem to follow, but he would understand the restlessness of a congregation at such complete lack of co-operation among leaders in worship. Perhaps we shall pardon his anger when he discovers that the man in the pulpit dares to refer to himself as a prophet merely because he glories in the fact that he is a poor priest. The prophets have been the first to insist that religion has failed men so frequently because the pastors of people have failed to live up to the obligations of their office.

Not only did the prophets insist upon the necessity of sincerity in worship, but they recognized that the more elaborate the aids of religion became, the greater became the temptation to substitute the ritualistic act for religious living. Amos and Isaiah denounced in no uncertain terms the ceremonials of their day, for they noted that they had ceased to be roads over which man traveled in his search for communion with God; they were now acts which men performed for their own satisfaction and in the conviction that in so performing them they were meeting the whole obligation of religion. Here has been one of the great stumbling blocks of religion. It is still with us, for there are those who overembellish their services in the mistaken notion that an aesthetic thrill is an act of communion.

The prophets have done us great service in many areas, and not the least of these services has been that they have forced us to think clearly concerning the relationship between magic and worship. It has been a long, weary road over which men have traveled in this discovery, and there are still those who have not yet completed that journey. The goal has been reached by some; and though they will push on to further objectives, yet their shouts of delight at their new discoveries may cause the slower travelers to hasten in their journey.

8

The Long Expected Messiah

—————◆—————

THERE WERE THREE GREAT FACTS WHICH CAME TO BE FIRMLY established in the Hebrew mind by the close of the Persian period that were essential to a messianic expectation. The first of these was the reality of God. The priestly writer's magnificent poem of creation (Gen. 1:1–2:4) indicates this conviction, "In the beginning God created the heavens and the earth." The significance for the Hebrew lay in the absolute sovereignty of God. Even in the earlier days of Hebrew history when Yahweh was thought to be the sole property of the Hebrew people, no question was raised concerning the origin of God; his pre-existence was everywhere taken for granted. When we come to the teachings of Jesus concerning the relationship of God and man, we do not find him taking time to argue the existence of God. That was taken for granted.

The second great factor was the belief in man's unique creation. He had been created by God and believed himself to be the lord of creation. "Then God said, 'Let us make man in our image, after our likeness, and let him have dominion over the fish of the sea, the birds of the air, the domestic animals, the wild beasts, and all the land reptiles!'" (Gen. 1:26.) Man has been created in God's image. What is the element that differentiates man from the animal? A physical concept of God was not prominent in the late Persian period, at least not in the minds of the more learned with whom the priestly writers may properly be associated. The likeness in this record was quite probably in a spiritual or intellectual sense. Self-conscious reason was the differentiating element. It was this power that made it possible for man to commune with God. Man had been given power to rule on the earth, and this was an indication that God had given him special attention. It was believed that it was this fact that made it possible for man to live in harmonious relation with

God. In the story of creation from an earlier period man alone received the "breath of life" from Yahweh (Gen. 2:7). On the basis of this and similar statements man was conceived to be the crown of creation, and there was peace between God and man.

Into this harmonious relation came discord. Instead of using his powers in harmony with divine expectation, man used them contrary to that expectation. Man therefore forfeited his right to communion with the Deity. As sin came in, man moved away from God. There was a growing conviction that the inevitable result of sin was separation from God. The religious leaders said that the divine purpose is right relations between God and man. If God overlooks sin, either he is unable to overcome it or he is unconcerned. Either is bad, for a righteous God must overcome sin in the world. The ultimate hope in the Old Testament expressed by the prophets and priestly writers alike is the re-establishment of communion with God.

The third presupposition, then, was a profound conviction that the original plan of Yahweh would be carried to completion in spite of man's sin. Throughout the Semitic world there was similarity of thought. Men saw about them evidences of the constant struggle between the forces of righteousness and the forces of evil. Men always identified themselves and their particular God with the forces of righteousness. A day was coming when all the forces of evil would finally be overcome and the nation and its God of righteousness would live in tranquillity forever. In the days of Amos the Hebrews talked optimistically of the coming day of the Lord, and the people believed that politically and economically they were to be led to victory. Another writer stated that Yahweh-Elohim would put enmity between man and the serpent, therefore between man and temptation (Gen. 3:15). Later writings made the serpent the personification of sin, but it was not until the Wisdom of Solomon that the serpent was identified with Satan. By that time Satan was identified as the leader of the forces of unrighteousness, and now the cosmic struggle was between God and Satan; but whatever the form of the struggle or whatever the identity of the opposing forces, it was the profound conviction of man that righteousness would ultimately triumph and God's purposes prevail.

In its broadest sense Messianism is the expectation that the kingdom of God will be established and shall prevail. The form of that kingdom and the identity of the controlling power in that kingdom have been variously interpreted, and this has led to confusion.[1] Orthodox Jews still look for the coming of a descendant of the line of David who shall sit upon David's throne and re-establish a political empire. The Reformed Jews look for the coming of a day when Jewish ideas, ethics, and power shall become the great controlling factors in the world. Among the early Christians there was no unanimity of opinion. In the Synoptic Gospels, Jesus is nowhere referred to as "Messiah," that term being applied to him only in the later Gospel of John (1:41; 4:25). The Greek term *Christos,* meaning "the anointed," is used far more frequently in the epistles than in the Gospels. There is disagreement in Christian circles today whether the Kingdom is God's rule in the hearts of men or is that Kingdom to be established on the earth after the Second Coming. Further confusion in thought arises from the fact that in Christian circles an identification has been made among the Messiah, the Servant, and the messianic Agent, identification that is not to be found in Jewish writings. The attempts to read back into Hebrew concepts and terminology the patterns that were developed later in Christianity have prevented us from recognizing that the Christian concept of the Messiah is totally different from the Hebrew conception. Confusion is still with us because so many Christians have not moved away from the old Jewish picture to the more noble picture which Jesus gave of the kingdom of God. An understanding of the road over which man has traveled in his search for a Messiah and the kingdom of God should enable us to separate the wheat from the tares.

The Hebrews have believed from very early times that there has been a special relationship between Yahweh and their particular national group. After the flood according to the priestly record Yahweh confined his relations among men to the Hebrew people. The earlier Judean record announced the coming of a promise to Abram that his descendants should become a great nation, and that he and the nation were to be the agents through which the earth should be blessed (Gen. 12:1-3). He

[1] John Bright, *The Kingdom of God* (New York and Nashville: Abingdon Press, 1953).

was to migrate from Haran and journey to a new land which Yahweh had designated for him and for his people. The Hebrews never looked upon themselves as conquerors or invaders but always as possessors of a divine inheritance.[2] Abram and the nation descended from him were to be the means of bringing about the perfect relationship between Yahweh and men.

The whole nation was too unwieldy a group with which to work, and quite early in history a narrowing process began. After the demise of Abraham, Isaac was the recipient of divine favor and promise, then Jacob. From the tribe of Jacob, Judah was selected to be the leader of the group. He was strong as a lion and so prosperous that he could wash his garments in wine. His eyes were bloodshot with wine and his teeth white with milk. This picture of material prosperity is constantly recurrent in messianic expectation.

The Great Unknown Prophet of the Exile, writer of the latter half of the book of Isaiah, enlarges the theme. He brings a challenge that has not been felt before. Once more it is the nation that is portrayed as the agent of Yahweh. Charles C. Torrey calls Isa. 42:1–43:7 "the great contrast." [3] On one side is a picture of the perfect servant as designed in the mind of God. On the other side is the picture of the servant as he actually is. It is Yahweh's purpose that the servant, the nation Israel, shall function in accord with the promise to Abram. It is the nation as a group, not a specially selected individual from that group, who shall be the means of bringing men to God.

With the establishment of the Hebrew kingdom it was natural for the king to have great significance. In the past Yahweh had led the people to battle. Now through their new leader the king they were to overcome the enemies of Yahweh and of Israel. The king had taken over the part that had formerly been played by Yahweh. The promise of the continuation of the dynasty of David, then, is of real significance (II Sam. 7:11-12), for without the leadership of a monarch the nation could not go forward with its task of overcoming the Gentiles. The promise was given also that the relationship between Yahweh and the king was to be particularly intimate. The

[2] The Hebrews did not accept the term "Hebrew," which originally meant "invader," until a very late date; and then they rationalized it to mean "one who crossed over."

[3] *Second Isaiah* (New York: Chas. Scribner's Sons, 1928), pp. 135 ff.

throne was to be firmly established.[4] The Hebrew, therefore, thought of his nation as the peculiar agent of Yahweh. The group was narrowed to Jacob and to the tribe of Judah. The king was to be the leader of the people, but he was to be descended from the tribe of Judah. It was through the king that the great kingdom of God was to be established.

How, when, and where the messianic kingdom was to be established are important questions to which much attention is given throughout Hebrew writings. According to Isaiah (2:2-4) there were four important conditions which were to be fulfilled. First, Jerusalem was to be the center of the kingdom. This was in agreement with the old Hebrew nationalistic hopes and expectations. In other respects the prophet differed from the later developments of the kingdom idea. Isaiah states that Yahweh himself was to be the ruler of the kingdom. There was no reason for a separate messianic king or leader. Yahweh would rule with moral influence. That would be the thing that would attract. There was apparently no thought given to the function of a mediating priesthood. The people would approach God directly. A final condition was that there would be no national supremacy. All nations were to be on an equal footing. They would come directly to Yahweh and not through the mediation of Israel. This does not mean that Israel would not be the agency through which they could find God; but it does suggest that after the Gentiles should have found God, Israel would have no distinction from other people. Elsewhere Isaiah addressed his message to the "survivors of Israel" (4:2-6). They were a purged remnant, and they "will be called holy," for all pollution was wiped away.

Jeremiah (31:31-34) longed for a time when people would not have to be informed concerning God, for all would know him most intimately. Instruction would no longer be necessary. But in his description of the Kingdom it is only for the "house of Israel and . . . the house of Judah." There is no internation-

---

[4] There is a probable connection between the messianic king and a belief among some Hebrews in divine kingship. Cf. Williams, *American Journal of Semitic Languages*, LI, 240; J. M. P. Smith, "Traces of Emperor Worship in the Old Testament," *American Journal of Semitic Languages*, XXXIX (1922), 32-39; and C. W. McEwan, *Oriental Origin of Hellenistic Kingship* (Chicago University Oriental Institute Studies in Ancient Oriental Civilization, No. 13) (University of Chicago Press, 1934).

alism here. It is to be noted, however, that there is but one way in which the new relationship can come, and that is the disappearance of sin, for it is that which has caused the separation. Therefore sin is to be removed and forgotten. Religion is considered in terms of individual moral responsibility and not in national terms, hence the change in the concept of the Kingdom.

In the postexilic period a number of additions were appended to the messages of the prophets. They are significant, for they indicate the changing aspects of the kingdom in postexilic thought. In Amos 9:11-15 the great change associated with the day of the Lord is discussed. This passage differs from the original picture given by Amos. This is a return to the old nationalistic ambition. The remnant is to become a new great nation. The old dynasty of David is to be restored and will furnish leadership for the new kingdom. A second feature is the reconquering of the surrounding peoples, so that the territory is to be as great as "in the days of old." Extraordinary fertility is to be one of the pleasures of that new day. A very rapid harvest will result. An important element is the permanent establishment of the righteous nucleus in the chosen land of Palestine.

In Hos. 2:14-23 not only are great fertility and a very intimate relation between God and man portrayed, but a peace shall pervade the earth that shall include all animals. They will no longer be antagonistic to man.

Joel pictures not only a time of great prosperity but a restoration of all that has been lost during the time of adversity. All that had been lost and destroyed when the land was overrun with locusts will be made good. Prosperity will be so great that the barns will be scarcely big enough to hold the harvest.

The elements that seem to predominate in most writings then are these: Israel will be the center of the new kingdom, Jerusalem will be the center within that kingdom, great prosperity will attend the efforts of the Israelites, and peace will pervade the earth.

The term "messiah" is used almost without exception in the Old Testament to indicate the king. There was an anointed priesthood, and it is altogether possible that the prophets were anointed to office, but *the* messiah, the noun form with the definite article, always indicated the king. Emphasis shifted from time to time, and during the period of the Exile less emphasis was placed upon the messianic king. At the end of the Exile the great unknown prophet saw in Cyrus of Persia new hope for Israel and saw in him an instrument through which the Hebrews could be restored to their own land. He therefore dared to call Cyrus the Lord's Messiah (Isa. 44:28; 45:1). In the postexilic period, when the Hebrews were nothing but a buffer state without political autonomy, emphasis was put upon ecclesiastical leadership.

Changes in thought were inevitable because of changing political fortunes. But certain fundamental points are uniform concerning the messianic king. He is to be a descendant of the dynasty of David.[5] He is to rule over an earthly kingdom with Judah as the people and Jerusalem as the center. The king is to be endowed with superhuman qualities of character, of spiritual nature, of wisdom; and he is to be an idealized reflection of the great historical hero David. The character of his reign is to be unusual, for he will be particularly interested in the poor and needy. All accounts teach that he will come in the near future. The more strained and troubled the national situation became, the more intense became the desire for the coming of the messianic king.

It is to be noted that there is never an identification of the messianic king with the Suffering Servant. In the only writing that discusses both (the latter part of the book of Isaiah) it is clear that the two are not identical. Although Isa. 44:28 identifies Cyrus as messiah, the king through whom Yahweh will bring political restoration, it is likewise clear throughout that document that the servant is the nation. In Isa. 44:21 Israel is identified as the servant. Four interpretations have been offered in answer to the question regarding the identity of the servant in the various servant songs: the nation Israel, a portion of Israel, an individual, the ideal Israel. The probable answer to the question is that all except the third were in the mind of the writer.

[5] With the possible exception of Ps. 110, where identification is made with family of Melchizedek not the family of David.

The nation Israel had been commissioned with the task, but only a portion of the nation underwent the experience of the Babylonian exile, and it is an interpretation of this grueling experience with which the prophet is concerned. It is likewise true that the only Israel that can measure up to the expectation of God is that Israel which is idealized in the mind of the prophet. He is urging contemporary Israel to meet the challenge of those specifications, and it is possible to see in the fifty-third chapter how the prophet swings in his thinking from the whole nation to the purged remnant. In that chapter it is the ideal Israel who is the servant, but at times the writer addresses the whole nation Israel as if they had come up to his expectations and have accepted the challenge that has been thrown out to them. If the writer is at all consistent, then we should expect that the servant is identical in all the servant songs. We shall assume that he is consistent. In 42:1-7 the unique character of the servant is portrayed. He has a divine commission; for, "I have put my spirit upon him," says Yahweh. We will not be a man of war but a man of peace. His method will not be that of forcing an issue but one of moral and spiritual instruction. He will be in close contact with all peoples. After these qualifications have been given, the prophet pictures Yahweh turning to the nation Israel with the words:

I the Lord have called you in righteousness,
And have grasped you by the hand;
I have kept you, and have made you a pledge to the people,
A light to the nations.

(Isa. 42:6).

Again, in Isa. 49:1-7 the challenge is thrown out to the nation Israel: "You are my servant, Israel"; but the servant is to carry a message, not to his own people, but to other nations. It is too slight an honor to be appointed as the servant of Yahweh merely for the purpose of carrying the message to Israel. The larger task of carrying the message to all peoples must be accepted. This is the prophet who interpreted the sufferings of the Exile as preparation for a greater task and likewise that others should not similarly suffer. His message of the principle of vicarious suffering is one of the great concepts of all time, and it has come to have a large place in the later Christian teachings concerning the work and mission of the Messiah. This prophet kept separate the tasks of the Messiah and the Suffering Servant; Christianity has identified them. In the light of the work and teaching of Jesus it has been the judgment of history that the only way in which the kingdom of God can be established is through vicarious suffering, that the only individual worthy of the title "The Lord's Anointed" is the one who made himself servant of all.

The Psalms give us the most intimate understanding of personal religious hope and expectation in the Bible. Many writers have seen in the Psalms a foretelling of the coming Messiah. It should be remembered, however, that the Psalms are not prophecy in any sense of the term but are lyrics of the national poets. We can see in them the hopes and dreams of the community because they found their way into the accepted body of scripture only because the people gave their approval. Yet they do not give a consistent picture of messianic expectation. They are prayers, and in many of them there is a cry that the Kingdom might be established (7, 13, 22, 35, 57, 59, 68, 74, 83, 85, 90, 94, 106-9, 115, 123, 126, 130, 144). Some of the Psalms think definitely in terms of a Davidic kingdom that is to be re-established (18, 72, 89). Not a few of them look forward to the coming of the Kingdom without any particular responsibility on the part of the Deity; it is to come largely through the efforts of man (60, 69, 75, 77, 96, 102, 113, 135, 138, 140, 149). In others the whole responsibility rests upon God (29, 97, 99, 110). In at least three of the Psalms the judgment is portrayed as being in progress at the time of the writing of the psalm (18, 58, 82), while in others the judgment is definitely in the past (2, 24, 46, 47, 48, 76, 93, 98).

Despite these discrepancies there is a consistent testimony concerning the popular expectation. There is an undying loyalty to Yahweh as the God of righteousness; Israel has a divine mission which is to result in a world-wide establishment of righteousness; religion is identified with national hopes, not with individual desires, and any expectation for the future is to be realized by the nation not the individual; and finally, there is a conviction that the ideals of love, right, truth, cannot be es-

112

tablished without miraculous intervention. The final patterns of messianic expectation in the period immediately before the coming of Christianity are a turning away from the dreams of the prophet with his faith in the dignity of human endeavor. Now a pessimism has crept in that completely despairs of human conduct and believes that God alone can establish the kingdom of God. The contrast between the prophet's expectations and the despair of the later writers known to us as "apocalyptists" is sharp. These contrasts are significant, for they have continued to exist in the centuries since.

Jesus was truly in the succession of the prophets, and all attempts to superimpose the pessimism of the apocalyptists upon his teachings have resulted in chaotic thinking among Christians and a defection from the message of Jesus and his program. To be sure, Jesus was influenced by the expectation in his own day; but he turned against the old nationalistic and pessimistic pattern at so many points that it is fair to assume that he rejected the general picture of messianic expectation that was prevalent in his day.

In those centuries immediately preceding the birth of Jesus there developed a type of literature that was largely new to the Hebrews but that gave large place to messianic expectation. It was a crisis literature wholly different from the messages which the prophets delivered in times of crisis. The pattern has been retained in Christianity and has appeared in a number of guises, but always there is the same underlying pattern of thought. The Millerites of the nineteenth century and the followers of Karl Barth in the twentieth are but two of many movements in recent times belonging to the crisis group. The apocalyptist, like the prophet, wrote in times of crisis for the purpose of strengthening faith. Professor R. H. Charles calls it a Semitic philosophy of religion, but there is no more reason for calling the writing of the apocalyptist a philosophy than the work of the prophet. Both are attempts to come to grips with the great problems of life.

The apocalyptic writings are prevailingly, though not necessarily, anonymous. They have been labeled "pseudepigraphic," but the writers had no intention of committing forgery; they simply used pen names. The reason is obvious. Because of the absolute supremacy of the law in this period, there was no room for further prophecy in spite of the fact that the law indicated that God would always deliver messages through the prophets. The only way in which the writers of these messages of encouragement could get them read was to give their words authority by appealing to antiquity. As a matter of fact there was little new in these writings. The authors were content to bring new and sometimes fantastic interpretations to the long-known words of the prophets.

Apocalyptic writings were primarily concerned with the hereafter, whereas the prophets were concerned about the here and now. The prophets emphasized that the kind of world God had planned would come if men would bring their lives into harmony with the fundamental principles of God, and the new age was an outgrowth of the present age. The writers of the apocalypses looked for the new age; but it would come only with the cutting off of the present age, which they believed was completely in the power of Satan; and the new age would come as the result of the intervention of God, not through human activity. These writers looked for a sudden and immediate end to the present age. The change was to be announced by a complete upheaval of nature and a thorough disruption of the normal processes of nature. The apocalyptist dispenses completely with human endeavor, though curiously enough some of the crisis theologians have been among the most active evangelists.

They fail to see that there is a fundamental contradiction between the two. Their faith is pinned to the hereafter, for they are wholly pessimistic concerning the present. The prophet cried for the repentance of the nations; but he believed sincerely that because he had delivered his message, men would repent, lives and society would be changed, and God's purpose would be established and find its expression in a moral society. The apocalyptist said that his message came to him through visions and supernatural revelation, but the prophet drew his message from normal events that surrounded him day by day and from his sense of companionship with God through his prayer life.

Protestantism denied a place in the canonized Scriptures to the apocryphal writings, most of which are apocalyptic; but it has been inconsistent in allowing apocalypticism to become dominant in two important areas of religious instruction. First of all, we have allowed the later character of the apocalyptist to displace the forthright and rugged picture of the prophet. Most of the popular definitions held by people of a prophet would more accurately describe the work of the apocalyptists. That is unfortunate. Whether we are in sympathy with the work of the apocalyptists or not, it is tragic that the far different picture of the work of the prophets should have been forgotten. Historical study of Hebrew religion has helped us to recover that magnificent picture. Likewise, we have all too readily accepted the apocalyptist's picture of the end of the world, the coming judgment, and the establishment by supernatural means of a kingdom which shall be forced upon men, instead of stressing the teaching of Jesus that God's kingdom comes as men follow his teachings and bring their lives into harmony with the moral law of God.

Not only is the Christian understanding of the kingdom of God vastly different from the old Jewish idea, but the Christian teaching concerning the function of the Messiah is completely at variance with the Old Testament position. It was the task of the Hebrew Messiah to bring about the establishment of a kingdom which was predominantly political. He was to bring material prosperity and abundant fertility. The whole thought pattern was in terms of old nationalistic ambitions. Christianity has completely changed this picture. The function of the Messiah is to bring men as individuals into right relation with God. No thought is given to the work of the Messiah with the social group, whether as a nation or a group of nations. At times the picture has included a judgment scene in which the Christ is a substitutionary sacrifice, but this sacrifice is paid for men as individuals, not en masse.

Many of our evangelistic songs have been sickeningly sentimental, but always there is the note that redemption is for the individual, not for society. The Christian has believed that as his life was changed by the challenge of the teachings of Jesus and brought into harmony with moral law, his changed life, in cooperation with others so changed, would result in a changed society. His great concern has been, not for a changed society per se, but for the benefits that would result to the individuals in that society. Here is a full rounding out of the message of the prophets. They built their hope upon the dignity of man, the divine element within man that could be challenged. Man came to see under the insistence of the prophets that the very essence of religion is man's personal responsibility to God. What was more natural then that the final interpretation of messianic hope should be in terms of a Messiah who should be concerned for the salvation of individuals.

9

National or Personal Immortality?

————◆————

IT IS NORMAL FOR ANYONE TO BE CONCERNED NOT ONLY ABOUT his present life but also with the problem, what will happen to him after death. The neighbors of the Hebrews were concerned; and while there is no clear-cut teaching concerning personal immortality in the Old Testament, there is much evidence that the Hebrews had definite convictions about what happened to them in death.

Sheol was the abode of all the dead. The terms "Sheol" and "death" are used interchangeably.

> Shall I rescue them from the power of Sheol?
> Shall I redeem them from death?
> Where are your plagues, O Death?
> Where is your destruction, O Sheol?
> > (Hos. 13:14.)

The common method was to speak of going to Sheol rather than to say that one would die.

> I must go hence in the noontide of my days,
> And be consigned to the gates of Sheol for the rest of my years.
> > (Isa. 38:10.)

There was no distinction. All went to Sheol. Death was not an extinction but a continuation of life in another place, in a shadowy reproduction of the events of this life in a world that was forever dark. The nation was intact there, so it was natural to think of joining those who had gone before. Again and again we find the expression, "He was gathered to his fathers" (Gen. 25:8, *et al.*). Abraham, Jacob, Aaron, and other leaders of the people were in Sheol; but so was Ishmael, who had a lesser reputation. Even the stillborn child and the abortioned fetus (Job 3:16) went to Sheol. It was taken for granted that if a man died, he went there.

> What man can live and not see death,
> Can deliver himself from the power of Sheol?
> (Ps. 89:48.)

The Hebrew believed in a three-storied universe—the heavens above, the earth beneath, and the waters under the earth (Exod. 20:4) —with Sheol either in the waters under the earth or in the bowels of the earth itself. The next question which naturally presents itself is, How was Sheol reached, and who went there?

Sheol was the Semitic equivalent of the classical conception of Hades. It was the final abode of all the departed. Its location was under the waters that are under the earth.[1] It was beneath the foundations of the mountains, for the utter wrath of Yahweh is described as reaching to the farthest depths of Sheol and setting on fire the foundations of all the mountains (Deut. 32:22).

The Hebrews used it to denote one extremity of the universe. In the chapter on the glorification of wisdom Job implies the far-reaching power of Yahweh's wisdom by making Abaddon, a synonym for Sheol, say, "We have but heard the report of it." (28:22).

The entrance to Sheol is by means of gates (Isa. 38:10). These gates must have been bolted, for we read of the bars of Sheol. The number of gates is not mentioned, but here is another suggestion that the writer may have been influenced by the Babylonian concept.

The picture of Sheol is not an enticing one, and even a man in utter despair finds it anything but an inviting place. It is a dark and dismal cavern. In Proverbs we read of the "chambers of death." The plural is often used by the Hebrews to denote size or grandeur, and such is the case here. The phrase would therefore be more accurately translated "The Great Chamber of Death." Another synonym for Sheol is the "Pit" (Job 17:14; Ps. 55:23; Ezek. 32:18, 24).

---

[1] See O. R. Sellers, "Israelite Belief in Immortality," *The Biblical Archaeologist*, VII, No. 1 (Feb. 1945), 1-16.

Sheol is

> a land of shadow, like gloom,
> Of blackness without order,
> And when it shines, it is like gloom.
> (Job 10:22.)

It is a land of dust (Job 17:16). According to the Babylonian literature even the food of the departed was dust. Dust lay upon the doors and the bolts of the doors. Such evidently is the thought of the book of Job.

Since Sheol was somewhere beneath the earth, it became quite natural to think of the grave as the entrance to Sheol. Therefore man had to be buried, either naturally or unnaturally, in order to reach the place of the departed. There was the possibility of reaching Sheol alive, but only in the case of a sudden eruption of the earth caused by God's anger. In Numbers there is a graphic description of such a situation:

> But if the Lord does something new, and the ground opens its mouth, and swallows them up, with all that belongs to them, and they descend into Sheol alive, then you shall know that these men have despised the Lord.
>
> And then, just as he finished saying these words, the ground under them split open; the earth opened its mouth and swallowed them up, with all their households, and all the men who belonged to Korah and all their goods. So they and all that belonged to them descended into Sheol alive; and the earth closed over them, and they perished from the community. (16:30-33.)

An opening up of the earth was looked upon as an opening to Sheol, which was thought to be a yawning pit.

> Therefore Sheol has enlarged her appetite,
> And opens her mouth without limit.
> (Isa. 5:14.) [2]

> There are three things that are unsated,
> Four that never say, "Enough":
> Sheol, and the barren womb,
> The earth unsated with water;
> And fire that never says, "Enough."
> (Prov. 30:15b-16.)

[2] Ehrlich says that the idiom also means to enlarge capacity.

Within Sheol existence is a dreary reflection of life on the earth. It is a land of forgetfulness, of nerveless, ineffective existence, a land of eternal sleep (Job 3:17-19). Silence reigns supreme. The inhabitants are called *repha'im*, meaning "shades," relaxed or flaccid ones, mere resemblances of their former selves. It was a land of no return.

In the Holiness Code (Lev. 17–26) there is a command: "Do not turn to mediums or magicians; do not defile yourselves with them by consulting them, since I, the Lord, am your God" (19:31). This is followed in the next chapter with a statement of the punishment of such practices: "If any person turns to mediums and magicians by running wantonly after them, I will set my face against that person, and cut him off from his people" (20:6). There were two causes for these precautions. The first was to prevent worship of the dead. Yahweh alone was God, and to him alone must the people turn for advice in all matters of life. God had promised that there should always be a means of knowing his will, a prophet like unto Moses (Deut. 18:15-18). The prophets recognized that it was proper to seek to know the will of God (Isa. 8:19), and that was prophetic function, but necromancers had gone a step further and said that it was proper to seek to know the will of God by any means, legitimate or otherwise.

Necromancers and wizards had developed certain practices to know the will of Yahweh. Those who had the superior power of knowing Yahweh's will upon the earth were thought to retain that knowledge in Sheol. This probably was the basis for necromancy. It was for this reason that we find Saul going to the witch of Endor and seeking to get into contact with the shade of Samuel (I Sam. 28:8-15). Saul thought that there might be some knowledge Samuel had failed to transmit while upon the earth. That Samuel actually appeared is indicated only by the witch, and there is nothing in the information that was imparted that she herself could not have given based upon the psychological study of Saul's condition. Thus the only story that we have of the appearance of a shade is not convincing.

The other reason for discountenancing the practice of necromancy was that Yahweh was thought for a long time not to have any power over Sheol. Thus if necromancers were able to cause the shades to rise, they would be exceeding the power of Yahweh.

Such a situation could not be tolerated. Not only was the practice of necromancy and wizardry condemned; but everyone connected with it, or even possessed of the power, whether practiced or not, was condemned (Lev. 20:27).

Aside from the magical purposes there could be no intercourse between the world of the living and the dwellers of the dust. King David bitterly mourned the loss of his son until he realized that such conduct could not cause the son to return. David must wait until he himself should go to Sheol, then there could be reunion.

Not only was there an impossibility of communication of the living with the dead, but it was impossible for the dead to know what was transpiring in the land of the living. In Job there is the picture of a man who has gone to Sheol. Even his most intimate contacts have been cut off. He cannot know the fortunes of his sons. Whether they come to honor or are plunged to the depths of shame, he cannot know of it.

Sheol was the "house appointed for all living" (Job 30:23 K.J.V.). Jacob would not be comforted for the loss of his son; he would go mourning to Sheol (Gen. 37:25). Evidently, then, whether faithful to the word of Yahweh or not, a man went to Sheol.

After his arrival there was there any distinction between the morally good and the morally bad? There was a social distinction, for kings sat upon thrones. The nations seem to have been segregated, for Ashur and her assembly were assigned to the remote parts of the pit (Isa. 14:9). But there was no moral distinction. All were together in a family group regardless of the lives they had lived. Men were not sent to Sheol to be punished. They were punished in being sent there. They were cut off from life and from relationship with God and man. Sheol held nothing in store for them, so that long life was the thing to be desired. It was thought that the good lived to a ripe old age and had prosperity, while the wicked suffered reversals and died young.

This is the thought of the psalmist when he says:

> For thy kindness toward me is great,
> In that thou hast rescued me from the depths of Sheol.
> (86:13.)

There is no thought here of a resurrection, not even an escape from going ultimately to Sheol. Evidently the psalmist has been in some great distress and God has spared his life. In his extremity he was close to Sheol, and in the removal of that distress he was saved from Sheol. The expression "depths of Sheol" shows how dire the experience was.

According to the earliest Hebrew conception Sheol stood outside Yahweh's authority. Yahweh was the God of the Hebrews, but they recognized that other nations had gods. Hence they held a rather limited view of the sway of Yahweh. If for any reason a man was forced to go out of the area over which Yahweh had power, that man was going away from the power of Yahweh. Just so, when a man died, he was removed from contact with Yahweh. In the Decalogue the command was given to "honor your father and mother" in order that life upon the earth in the land of the Hebrews may be long.

With the development of the concept of the power of Yahweh extension of the territory over which he held sway was inevitable. But even until a very late date the thought was, not that Yahweh was the ruler of Sheol, but that the reverberations of Yahweh's power could be felt in Sheol. Again and again the cry is made that death means the separation forever of God and man. With death comes the end of all communion. In Job, although the power of Yahweh is such that

> Sheol lies bare before him,
> And Abaddon has no covering (26:6),

yet Job cries:

Man expires, and where is he?
Water departs from the lake,
And a stream parches and dries up;
So man lies down and does not rise.
Until the heavens are no more they will not awake (14:10-12) —

that is, never.

In the exilic and postexilic Isaiah the thought is that with death comes permanent separation.

> Sheol cannot thank thee, death cannot praise thee;
> Those who go down to the Pit cannot hope for thy love.
>
> (38:18.)

The psalmist asks: "In Sheol who praises thee?" (6:6), then answers his own question by declaring that in death there is no remembrance of him.

In Ps. 88:6, 10-12, the psalmist pictures himself as one cast out, as those who had been slain, remembered no more by Yahweh and cut off from all contact with him. In despair he raises the questions:

> Is it for the dead that thou wilt do wonders?
> Will the ghosts arise to thank thee?
> Will thy kindness be recounted in the grave?
> Or thy faithfulness in Hades?
> Will thy wonders be made known in the darkness?
> Or thy righteousness in the land of oblivion?

He raises the questions knowing full well that the only answer is a negative one.

Again, in Ps. 115 three distinct divisions are made. The heavens are the realm of God, the earth was given by him to the sons of men, but the land of silence is for the dead and the dead shall not praise him.

In Ps. 139 another note is struck. The psalmist recognizes the far-sweeping power of Yahweh. If he ascends to heaven or makes his bed in Sheol, there Yahweh is. The psalmist does not mean that he feels there is a possibility of either ascending to heaven or going to Sheol, but he uses the expression as denoting the extremes of territory throughout which is felt the power of Yahweh.

The eighth-century prophets Amos and Hosea had expressed the same thought. Whether they dig into Sheol or ascend to heaven, Yahweh can still reach them. They cannot escape his presence. Hosea raises the questions

> Shall I rescue them from the power of Sheol?
> Shall I redeem them from death? (13:14.)

Each is answered by an emphatic No. Compassion is hid from Yahweh's eyes.

Only in the late book of Daniel is there the thought that Yahweh will extend his power to change the state of the dead and then only to reward the specially meritorious and to punish the reprobates. It suggests that both good and bad are in Sheol and that this is their proper place, and only under very exceptional circumstances does Yahweh have power to change from the regular procedure.

Until the rise of individualism from the teaching of Jeremiah and Ezekiel, the thought of Israel centered about the nation. It was with the nation that Yahweh had made his covenant. Israel as a nation would not be cut off. Yahweh had made his covenant with the nation through the house of David and not through David as an individual. We see in the early literature an emphasis upon the preservation of the nation through the propagation of children. It was an unfortunate thing for a woman to be barren, and for a man to be left without male heirs was thought to be a punishment from God. It was for this reason that the Levirate Law was formulated (Deut. 25:5-10). In the event that a man died and left no male descendants, his brother was to take his wife and raise seed to him. The first male child of the new union took the name of the deceased and was considered his child and heir. This was done so that there would be preservation of the family, and possibly to provide someone to tend the grave of the deceased. If the man refused to perform the obligations of the Levirate Law, his sister-in-law could cause him public disgrace; and the shame would rest upon him and his household forever.

It was because of this law that Boaz and Ruth hesitated about marriage (Ruth 4:5-6). Until the near kinsman had forfeited his claim, they could not be united. But when the near kinsman stated that he was unable to fulfill his obligations and signified his willingness to forego his rights by "loosing the sandal," then Boaz could take Ruth for himself. The significance for us in this passage is that here again is emphasis upon the national life. Without the propagation of children the nation could not last. National immortality consisted not in resumption of national life in a hereafter but in the continuation of the Hebrew nation upon the earth.

The account in Ezek. 37:1-14 has been taken to be a description of an actual miracle by the prophet. This interpretation is now doubted, and the question arises as to the significance of the vision, for such it was. Ezekiel himself records the purpose. It was a message from Yahweh. He envisions the people in captivity as being dead, at least as far as their national life is concerned. With the return of the people to Palestine and the resumption of national life, it would have been the equivalent of a resurrection. So he pictures the people of captivity as dead bones, their very dryness signifying the utter hopelessness of the situation. Then by a cataclysmic act Yahweh causes the "very dry" bones to become men of flesh and blood (Ezek. 37:7-10). In this act Ezekiel sees the return of the people from their now helpless position to their former place of significance as an independent nation.

It is true that Ezekiel had a message of individualism; and it is also true that as far as the future life was concerned, he had no hope for the individual; but the Hebrew people as a people would not die.

We see, therefore, that from the beginning of national life, and after the rise of individualism, no thought of resurrection was yet in evidence; but national immortality was plasmic.

Though a doctrine of resurrection was not formulated until a late date, there are hints in the early sources that man had in him a divine element that is immortal. Man naturally believes in immortality, as is evidenced by the fact that no primitive people have yet been found who believe that death is a total annihilation of life. The personality may be effaced by emergence with a greater power, or the existence may be nerveless, a shadowy reproduction of earthly life, but some form of continuance is recognized. It is only with the beginning of speculation that man begins to suspect that he might cease to be.

It is after such speculation had begun that the Bible stories of the creation were produced. The earliest account was written down sometime in the last part of the ninth or the beginning of the eighth century. In it an attempt is made to explain why it is that man does not have immortal life, since he is like unto God, "[knowing] good from evil." The emphasis has been placed by succeeding generations upon the origin of sin, whereas the real point of emphasis is upon the loss of eternal life. Man was sent from the garden, not primarily because of disobedience, but so that he could not obtain immortal life. It was a defense measure upon the part of Yahweh. Parallel stories, with similar defense by the deities, may be found in several ancient Near Eastern documents.

The later account was produced about 450 B.C. There was a less anthropomorphic conception of God. Man was created in the image of God. Therefore he had a divine element in him. Because of the fact that it was produced late, the growing conception of a possibility of an afterlife may have influenced the writer. The priestly writer gives no account of the fall of man.

Hebrew literature has two accounts of individuals who were thought not to have died. The oldest of these is the story of Elijah. Tradition says that he was taken to heaven in a chariot of fire (II Kings 2:11). The other account is another story from the pen of the priestly writer. Because of the good life of Enoch he was taken directly to heaven. "He disappeared; for God took him away." (Gen. 5:24.) Again, since it comes from a relatively late period, perhaps the diction, if not incident, is influenced by the developing thought regarding life after death. There is justification for believing that upon the basis of these stories psalmists hoped that their lives might be so intimately connected with Yahweh, that their lives might be so good, that they too could be taken to be with him as were these men.

There are two problems that seem to be uppermost in the minds of the psalmists. First is the problem of good and evil. Throughout the Psalms is expressed the intense personal relation that can exist between God and man. But the rise of the doctrine of individualism brought with it a new problem. What of the justness of God? If Sheol is for all with no punishment for evil or reward for good, what of the righteous man who has had adversity or has been cut off in the prime of life, and what of the sinner who has had prosperity or lived to a ripe old age? The psalmists are constantly wrestling with the problem. The prosperity of the righteous and the punishment of the wicked are pleaded and longed for. In Ps. 37 the writer begins: "Fret not yourself because of evildoers." Why? "For evil doers shall be cut off."

> "Yet a little while and the wicked shall be no more;
> Though you look hard at his place, he will not be there."

Later in the psalm we are cautioned to

> watch integrity and look upon right;
> For there is a posterity for the man of peace.
> But lawbreakers are wholly destroyed;
> The posterity of the wicked is cut off.

The psalmist here makes no reference to life after death. He is thinking only in terms of a long life for the righteous and a short one for the wicked. Again, in Ps. 16 we have an expression of the highest faith in Yahweh:

> Thou wilt not abandon me to Sheol;
> Thou wilt not let thy godly one see the Pit.

This expression of confidence is determined by the psalmist's deep sense of communion with God. But experience did not bear out the hope that the wicked would be punished with a short life and the righteous rewarded by a long life. Good men still continued to die, and the wicked still continued to prosper. The psalmist answered this by showing that the highest thing in life was communion with God. This the righteous man had, but the wicked man had not.

> But I in justification shall behold thy face;
> I shall be satisfied when thy form awakes.
> (Ps. 17:16.)

The other great problem, then, that confronted the psalmists was the relation of God and man. To them this was the great punishment, that in death man was to be cut off from communion with Yahweh. J. Y. Simpson states, "It is important, therefore, to note that the Old Testament is not really interested in personal immortality except so far as that involves a personal relationship to God." [3] This is the position of the psalmists certainly. Life is dear only so far as God is near to them. They are content to let the future wait. Robert Louis Stevenson said, "To believe in immortality is one thing, but it is first needful to believe in life." The psalmists believed so

[3] *Man and the Attainment of Immortality* (New York: Harper & Bros., 1922), p. 279.

thoroughly in life that at times it seems that the future was forgotten.

Throughout the Psalms there is no definite expression of a belief in a future life. There is hope. But the great concern is for the continuation of the present close relationship between Yahweh and man upon the earth. "There is none upon earth that I desire beside Thee." (Ps. 73:25.)

From the book of Job expressions epitomizing the Christian faith have been culled. "If a man dies, does he live?" (14:14*a*). "Yes" has been the answer of the Christian Church, but it certainly was not Job's. Properly translated, the question should give the sense, "If a man dies, he certainly isn't alive, is he?" "I know that my redeemer liveth" (19:25 K.J.V.) has been taken as the theme of one of the great anthems of the Church, but here again we have taken words from a translation colored by Christian theology and not the thought of Job. At least according to the beginning of Job's story it does not appear to be, for he fully expects to go to Sheol (3:13-19). He is utterly weary of life; he is tired from the struggle and looks for rest.

> There the wicked cease from troubling;
> There the weary are at rest.

The utter hopelessness of the situation is revealed in the following speech. He is as a cloud consumed.

> So is the one who descends to Sheol; he will not ascend.
> He will not return again to his house;
> Nor will his place know him again.
>
> (7:7-10.)

Once he has gone to Sheol, there is no hope for him; for he is utterly cut off from Yahweh. Restitution must be made on earth. His friend had reprimanded him for his complaint in chapter 3. In chapter 6 Job defended himself; and now his complaint naturally turns to Yahweh, whom he holds responsible for his present condition. Unless Yahweh comes to the rescue and vindicates him before his friends, Job's character will be blemished forever; for after death there is no chance of vindication.

Again, in chapter 14 Job looks for hope. There is hope for a tree. If it is cut down, it will sprout again. The smell of water, faint as it is, will revive it. But alas, such is not the case with man. Man lies down in death, and where is he? Once he dies, that is the end. He will lie there forever. Verse 14*a* is either out of place or is an interpolation. It interrupts the thought; but in any case the question, "If a man dies, does he live?" must be answered with an emphatic *No*. There is no hope. Verse 14*b* continues the thought of verse 13. If there were any hope at all, Job would be willing to wait. If he thought that Yahweh could hide him in Sheol until his vindication, he would be satisfied. The unbearable thing is to suffer the condemnation of his friends when he knows very well that he has not sinned and that the punishment is unjustified. Something has gone wrong with the eternal laws; but if there were a possibility of their being rectified and Job could be hidden until that time, then he would be happy.

"I know that my redeemer liveth." Has Job found an answer to his longings? It has been taken that he has and that his answer is that the vindication may not come within this life but that there is a life beyond, and in that life he may hope for acquittal. But this interpretation has been molded by Christian philosophy. Job has found an answer, but not in immortal life. The answer is clear. His redeemer, the Yahweh whom he had known through the years before the calamity came, would come to his rescue and vindicate him. It would be in this life, for it would be useless unless his friends could witness his vindication. So Job expresses complete confidence in Yahweh, but he gives no expression of belief in an uninterrupted individual eternal life.

It is through the book of Ecclesiastes that some scholars seek to establish proof that the Hebrew thought of a resurrection was greatly influenced by the Greeks. Therefore, it is important to see just exactly what Ecclesiastes has to say about life after death. Coming as it does from a late date, it would seem that the viewpoint should be rather fully developed.

Koheleth was an old man. He had sought the *summum bonum* of life and had been disappointed. He "saw under the sun that wickedness took the place of justice and wickedness took the place of righteousness" (3:16). Life had been a disappointment. Would a life hereafter answer the difficulty? Apparently it doesn't, for he writes that there is one circumstance to man and beast. As the one dies, so does the other. There is no difference. "Man has no advantage over the beast; for everything is vanity." (3:19.) There is a faint ray of hope in 3:17, but this verse is generally conceded to be an interpolation by a later scribe. Man and the beast are equal; they not only die the same, but they both are composed of the dust, and they shall return to the dust. There is no hope of immortality in that. Then he philosophizes: "Who knows whether the spirit of man goes upward and whether the spirit of the beast goes downward to the earth?" (3:21). The best answer that he can find is that there is nothing better than for a man to make the most of his opportunities here and rejoice in his work; for after he is dead, he cannot come back to rejoice in it.

A final statement comes from the last chapter.

> The dust returns to the earth as it was,
> And the spirit returns to God who gave it. (12:7.)

The spirit is evidently not the man himself but a loaned element from God to give life to the man, and at death it is returned to the giver. The man himself returns to the dust and is no more; for, "Futility of futilities," says Koheleth, in effect, "all is futility."

Whether or not Ecclesiastes was influenced by the Greeks seems to matter little as far as we are concerned in this particular problem, for there is no hope of future life in Koheleth.

Following the collapse of the nation and the crushing experience of the Exile, the individual had become the point of emphasis. Exilic prophets laid stress upon personal responsibility. It was only natural, then, that with the development of the idea of the resurrection the individual should be considered. Some would suggest that the idea started before the Exile and find in Hos. 6:1-2 a clear indication of this. But a closer examination of the passage will reveal that reference is not made to a resurrection. The prophet has been picturing the wrath of Yahweh. He will punish the people for their apostasy. He will rend, as does a lion; and there will be none to help. "Come, let us return unto the Lord." God has punished; but if the people will return to him, he will heal them. *Chayah* is to be translated in the sense not of raising from the dead but that Yahweh

130

will revive the people. The expression "after two days . . . : in the third" (6:2 K.J.V.) has been taken as foretelling the experience of Jesus, but it expresses nothing more than an indefinite but a short time before the fulfillment of the promise.

The first clear indication of a definite belief in individual resurrection is to be found in Isa. 26:19. The prophet is painting a picture of the day of Yahweh. He addresses Yahweh and ascribes all power and praise to him. Then comes the picture that on the day of Yahweh there shall be a resurrection. It is not national but individual, for "*thy* dead will live." Clearly the reference is to the Jews and to the good among the Jews. Yahweh is responsible for the resurrection, and the dew of lights is the immediate cause.[4] The dead are brought from Sheol, for they are now dwelling in the dust and the earth will cast them out. The picture comes to us from the end of the fourth or the beginning of the third century B.C.

In the book of Daniel, written during the second century B.C., a development is to be seen. Here again the resurrection is to be on the day of Yahweh. The resurrection is not general, but "*many* of those who sleep in the land of dust" shall awake. Apparently only the exceptionally good, or the martyrs in the conflict with the Greeks, and the apostates, are concerned. This passage reflects the feeling during the period of the conflict. There is development beyond Isaiah in the concept of the resurrection, for both the good and the bad are raised and come to their reward. Here again the dead are brought from Sheol. Some would suggest that there is reflected a decline in moral concepts, for the dead are raised to see the vindication of the righteous while the wicked suffer torment to the delight of the righteous, but this is not expressed by the passage.

Of these passages (Isa. 26:19 and Dan. 12:2) Albert C. Knudson says:

The two Old Testament passages which we have just considered belong to a late date. Daniel comes from the Maccabean period, and the apocalypse in Isa. 24–27 was probably not more than a century earlier. The late appearance of the doctrine of the resurrection in Israel naturally suggests the theory that the doctrine was bor-

---

[4] "Dew of herbs" is difficult to understand in this connection, and "dew of lights" has been accepted as preferable.

rowed from the Persians, with whom it originated earlier, and with whom the Jews had been in constant contact since the latter part of the sixth century. In favor of this theory not a little can be said. The resemblances between the Mazdean and the Jewish doctrine, especially in the form represented by Dan. 12:2, are manifest. Both teach a resurrection of the wicked as well as the righteous, and both connect it with the final Judgment. But along with these resemblances there are a number of points of difference. In one the resurrection is universal, in the other limited; in one the Judgment follows the Messianic era, in the other it precedes it; in one the departed go to their reward or punishment, heaven or hell, immediately after death, in the other they are all detained together in Sheol until the new era dawns.[5]

But it is doubtful if there is foreign influence, for the expressions are the natural development of Hebrew thought. It was at this period, too, that the Hebrews fought so hard against anything not Hebrew.

It is generally conceded that among all peoples there is a belief in some kind of immortality. The various beliefs may be grouped under three heads: belief in personal immortality; belief in influential immortality, as the Buddhists; and belief in plasmic immortality. As we have seen, the Hebrews belonged until a comparatively late date to the third group. They believed that national immortality was achieved through the propagation of children.[6] But by the time of Jesus thought had so changed that his teaching of personal resurrection did not fall on unprepared ground, and he was understood by his contemporaries. What were the reasons for this change?

The first factor responsible for a more ethical concept of life after death was a more ethical concept of God. In the early preprophetic period Yahwism was monolatry rather than monotheism. Yahweh was the God peculiar to the Hebrews. Other national gods were recognized. To go out of Canaan was to go away from Yahweh. Jacob was surprised to have a visitation of Yahweh while away from home. At death relation between God and man was cut off.

With the change from the nomadic life to that of the farmer

<hr>

[5] *The Religious Teaching of the Old Testament* (New York and Nashville: Abingdon Press, 1918), pp. 405-6. Used by permission of the publisher.

[6] Cf. W. O. E. Oesterley and T. H. Robinson, *Hebrew Religion, Its Origin and Development* (rev. ed.; New York: The Macmillan Co., 1937), pp. 79 ff.

and villager, a change came in the concept of God. It was indirect but nevertheless effective. As man came into closer relation with his fellow men, social ethics had to be higher, at least in theory. If in practice man fell below the standard, he had to be punished for the protection of society. With the elevation of standards for mankind the standards of Yahweh had to be elevated.

As Yahweh became more ethical than the surrounding gods, and the people became more nationalistic, he was conceived of as being more powerful. Gradually his power was extended until he was God of the whole earth but still retained Israel as his chosen people. At last there was no other god but Yahweh. Naturally when his power was world wide, he was also thought to have power over Sheol. Pre-exilic literature is lacking in extension of Yahweh's sway to Sheol (Isa. 38:10-11; Pss. 6:5; 88:5, 10; 115:17), but from the eighth century he is thought to have had authority over Sheol; at least his presence was felt there, although the place retained its old characteristics (Amos 9:2; Hos. 13:14; Ps. 139:7-8).[7]

With the emphasis upon the worship of Yahweh only, the worship of the spirits of the dead was forbidden; and Yahweh appropriated the cult of the dead. Rites of the dead that were not clearly acts of worship were still permitted, but they rendered the participator unclean. In the period of the prophets the activity of the dead was denied. Rites of mourning were restricted. All of this tended to make the power of Yahweh greater.[8]

During the Exile the worship of Yahweh by sacrifice was forbidden. The effect of this was to produce a more spiritual type of worship, which in its turn induced a higher concept of the spiritual relation between God and man. Another effect of the Exile was to emphasize the fact that Yahweh was not limited to Palestine, but his power extended even to Babylon. The combination of the power of Yahweh with a more ethical conception of the character of Yahweh provided the groundwork upon which could be built a high concept of life after death.

[7] See also Job 26:6 and B. Will, *Life After Death* (M. A. thesis, Northwestern University, 1915), p. 22.

[8] Paton, *Biblical World*, XXXV, 246 ff.

A second great factor responsible for the development in the thought regarding life after death was the rise of the doctrine of individualism. Here again the change from the nomadic life to the pastoral and urban life played its part. With a greater concourse of people the emphasis upon tribal and clan loyalty tended to decrease, and the individual came into more prominence. The commercial life was so constructed that emphasis was upon the individual rather than upon the tribe and clan. The establishment of a monarchical form of government, while it had a strong national emphasis, was not without its emphasis upon the individual.

The message of Jeremiah was to show the responsibility of the individual (31:30; cf. 31:33-34). Until now Israel had believed that the nation was the unit. The relation between Yahweh and Israel was on a national basis and not individual. The covenant was with the nation. Only in this way was it possible to account for the fact that the sins of fathers were visited upon the children to the third and fourth generation. But with the downfall of the nation and the beginning of the Exile, thought necessarily had to change. Either Yahweh was not as powerful as he had been thought to be, or the nation was not the unit. Ezekiel carried forward the message of Jeremiah (18:4, 30-32). If the individual was the important unit, then the relation between Yahweh and men could be personal. And this it was, as we have seen, for the psalmist.

With the development of priestcraft, too, there was necessarily a recognition of the individual. While the organization was primarily national, the individual could not be overlooked. It was with the individual that the priest had to deal. It was for him as well as for the nation that he had to officiate.[9]

One result of the rise of the doctrine of individualism was increased emphasis upon the problem of good and evil. The psalmists, Job, and Ecclesiastes wrestled with the problem. Experience did not endorse the theory that "piety equals prosperity." Sheol could not be the end. C. F. Burney points out that it was out of this speculation "that the idea of personal immortality appears to have arisen, at times as an aspiration or merely tentative solution of the anomalies and the present life,

[9] J. M. P. Smith, *American Journal of Theology*, X, 251 ff.

at times as a dearly prized conviction of individual hearts, but not yet as a definitely formulated dogma of religion." [10]

As was pointed out before, an even greater problem to the psalmists was that of the separation of man from Yahweh at the time of death. Life had become very important to the psalmist because of his contact with Yahweh. Would death end it all? The psalmists prayed for a long life in order that the relationship between them and God might be as long as possible; but at times there seemed to be a fervent prayer, a hope, that death might not end the companionship. It is interesting to note that it is the question of rewards and punishments that brings forth such thought as we have in Dan. 12:2, "And many of those who sleep in the land of dust shall awake, some to everlasting life, and others to everlasting reproach and contempt."

Three things, then, were necessary for the background of a high ethical concept of life after death: a high concept of the character of Yahweh, a recognition of the importance of the individual, and a sane approach to the problem of good and evil.

The Jewish belief in life after death gradually underwent change from the time of belief in a shadowy existence in Sheol to a belief in a resurrection of the body. The development was the result of two stimuli. One was a more ethical concept of God and man; the other was the attempt to provide a solution to the problem of good and evil. These were natural products of their experience. This much must be said for foreign influence: the fact that other religions had a belief in life after death may have stimulated the Jews to seek within their own for similar thought.[11] The evolution was bound to come, for the ultimate thought of reunion of God and man is a direct answer to the prayer of the psalmist. There is nothing in the thought of the resurrection as expressed in the Old Testament that is foreign to Hebrew thought. Whatever may be said for foreign influence, it cannot be maintained that a belief in an afterlife and a resurrection was the product of such influence. The thought evolved logically and naturally.

[10] *Israel's Hope of Immortality* (New York: Oxford University Press, 1909), p. 32.

[11] Cf. Abraham Kuenen, *The Religion of Israel to the Fall of the Jewish State,* tr. A. H. May (London: Williams & Norgate Ltd., 1874), III, 43.

One other factor needs to be considered. In the postexilic period an intense nationalism developed in Judaism. Additions to the writings of the prophets attest to the renewed hope for the nation, and much of the hope revolved around material prosperity and political triumph. Jerusalem was to be the political and religious center for all peoples. It was through the Jews that religious knowledge would come to mankind. Is it possible that the political and religious ambitions of the Jews were determining factors in the development of teachings concerning immortality? What more natural than to desire that the heroes and saints of Hebrew history should participate in the glories of Israel. Since that glory was to be manifest in a new kingdom to be established upon the earth, it was necessary that those participating should in some way be restored to the earth. Physical resurrection was therefore a necessity. (We should note that personal immortality and physical resurrection are not necessarily dependent each upon the other.) It is within later Judaism alone that we find the concept of a physical resurrection combined with the teaching of a kingdom of God upon the earth. The conclusion seems to be clear that postexilic nationalism dictated this particular combination.

10

God Speaks to Man

AN ENIGMA AT THE HEART OF RELIGION HAS BEEN THAT OF THE means of communication between God and man. If man is to be held morally responsible for failure or success in his attempts to bring his life into harmony with the divine will, then there must be some way in which he can discover what that divine will is. The twofold aspects of the problem are the age-old puzzles of revelation and of inspiration. The issue has been beclouded because men have insisted upon confusing "foretelling" and "foreseeing" with seeking to bring life into harmony with God's principles. Man has felt that in order to do God's will, he had to know what the future had in store for him and for his fellows. It is necessary, therefore, that we turn our attention first in this direction.

In the Mesopotamian valley in the lands of Babylon and Assyria men found answers to this problem that were satisfying at least to the religious soothsayers. A citizen of ancient Babylon who was confronted with this problem of ordering his life in conformity with the will of his God Shamash went to the Temple to discover what the desires of Shamash were. He took with him a sheep, which was then consecrated and slain. The sheep's body was immediately slashed open and its liver removed. All the secrets of the past and the future had been imprinted upon that liver. The only problem was to discover the key to the markings. For this contingency religious experts had prepared themselves. The information would be forthcoming upon the satisfactory payment of a fee, the offering of gifts, or some other suitable consideration. While the liver still quivered with warmth, its markings were read; and the inquirer governed his conduct accordingly.

Thousands of tablets are to be found in our museums today

137

giving exact information concerning correct procedures and interpretations in the profession of hepatoscopy. To make instruction of neophytes in this profession simpler, clay models of sheep's livers were prepared, and full information was appended concerning the various markings on the liver. It is quite probable that the Hebrews tried to guard against the inroads of this sorcery by providing in their law that whenever animals were offered in sacrifice, the coverings of the liver were to be burned immediately.[1]

Another technique followed by the ancients was that of watching the flight of birds, and during Roman times official observers were appointed by the government to interpret the prognostic significance of the movements of birds. Again, men listened intently to the sound of the wind in the trees, believing that such sounds were the whispering of the gods and that with the right key man could discover what the gods were planning for him. At least one story of this type of thinking has been preserved in biblical record. During David's war with the Philistines he sought guidance from Yahweh. The record says:

> You shall go up; go around to their rear and come upon them opposite the balsam trees. Then when you hear the sound of marching in the tops of the balsam trees, make haste, for at that moment the Lord has gone forth before you to fall upon the camp of the Philistines. (II Sam. 5:23-24.)

One technique that has been practiced by ancients and moderns is that of communication with the dead. The famous story of Saul's visit to the witch of Endor (I Sam. 28:3 ff.) is an excellent example of practices in the early days of the Hebrew monarchy. Its use by some moderns to prove that such communication is possible merely indicates that they have read this story without a knowledge of ancient beliefs and customs and with an inadequate understanding of human psychology. Saul was confronted by the Philistines, and true to the pattern of his day he hesitated to join battle without the knowledge that he was being led by the god of his people. He was unable to get satisfactory encouragement through the regular channels,

[1] See my *The Books of the Law* (New York and Nashville: Abingdon Press, 1945), p. 90.

and the prophet Samuel was dead. Saul therefore turned in desperation to a medium. He tried to cover up his movements by going in disguise, but it was so transparent that the woman had no difficulty in recognizing him, and at the psychologically correct moment she turned this knowledge to her advantage.

The greatest stock in trade in this profession has been a keen ability to read human nature. Without it one is doomed to failure. "Saul disguised himself by putting on other garments"; but considering that he had been chosen for his political leadership because of his physical stature, it would have been difficult for him to disguise merely by a change of clothing. He went "accompanied by two men." The ordinary man is not accompanied by a bodyguard, and the presence of these two men would indicate the importance of the man they accompanied. Then when the woman raised a question concerning her own safety if she should proceed with the séance, Saul could give her an answer of authority. Only the king or someone delegated by him had power to exonerate anyone for the violation of law. If by this time the witch of Endor did not know her client, then she was unfitted for her particular vocation.

Saul made it clear at once that it was Samuel with whom he wished to communicate, and this again simplified the task of the medium. The woman established contact, and it is revealing to note that it was the medium, not Saul, who saw Samuel. It is necessary also for us to recall that Saul believed that Samuel had not gone to heaven or into the presence of God, but was in Sheol. This is the reason that the record says clearly three times, "Bring *up* Samuel." Samuel had no new knowledge from Yahweh; Saul wanted merely to obtain the benefit of the knowledge that he was sure Samuel had had before his death. Suddenly, after having announced that she had made contact with Samuel, the woman shrieked, "Why have you deceived me, for you are Saul?"

Entirely unprepared for this revelation, Saul saw in this statement confirmation of the fact that this woman really knew her business. It is the same technique that is still used by the palm reader or gypsy, who having seen our initials on a handbag or tie clasp does not immediately announce her discovery but pretends later to read this information from our hands or the crystal ball. Saul became excited and asked, "What have you seen?" The woman said, "I have seen a divine being coming up out of the earth." "What was his appearance?" cried Saul. To which the woman replied, "An old man is coming up, . . . and he is wrapped in a mantle." From that detailed description Saul knew immediately that it was Samuel.

And what infomation did Saul derive from Samuel? Only the fact that on the morrow he would be defeated by the Philistines. He had been a defeated man when he first entered the presence of the woman, and it took no particular skill on her part to indicate that he would be defeated militarily the next day. In those days skill in battle was largely a matter of physical prowess. The king was a commander in chief who led his warriors in the fight, not one who stayed back at general headquarters. For Saul to go into battle afraid inevitably meant defeat, and the witch of Endor knew that. This story fits the general pattern of records of necromancy.

In the introduction to the Endor story it is indicated that Saul's method of seeking to uncover the future was illegal. Certainly the day came in Israel when only three means were considered legitimate: the interpretation of dreams, the drawing of lots or the reading of Urim and Thummim, and prophecy. Dreams were believed from very early times to have occult significance. As time passed, less and less attention was paid to dreams because men discovered it was so easy to arrive at many interpretations of the same dream.

In the early stories of the patriarchs frequent use was made of dream interpretation. There was enough psychological relation between the problems men faced and the dreams they dreamed that a natural association was made. Dreams can still be a useful guide to the psychiatrist who is seeking to uncover the tensions that lie hidden in the mind of his patient; but until man learned to analyze scientifically the processes of the mind, such value in dreams could not be discovered.

Until the psychoanalytic tool was developed, the interpretation of dreams was left entirely to charlatans. Any values that developed from the interpretation of dreams in ancient days were purely accidental discoveries or the ability of the interpreter to understand human nature. The most outstanding account is the experience of Joseph. His interpretation of the fat and lean cows enabled him to bring to the Pharaoh the solution of a problem that had long plagued that political leader. Joseph's solution, however, was not new. King Zoser had tried it nearly fifteen hundred years before Joseph proposed it.[2] Joseph's success lay in the fact that the interpretation of the story answered the tension that was in the mind of the Pharaoh. If it had not, Joseph and his interpretation would have been forgotten long ago.

The second recognized means of interpreting the will of the Deity was by the use of Urim and Thummim or other means of drawing lots. These were probably the names given to special stones used by the priests for consulting the oracle. One was the negative answer, the other the positive. When a Hebrew wanted to know the answer to a question that puzzled him, he went to the priest with it. The question had to be formulated so that it could be answered either negatively or positively. When the question was presented, the priest put the answer stones, Urim and Thummim, into his pouchlike apron, which was called an "ephod." After making the appropriate gestures and prayers, the priest put his hands into the ephod and drew out the answer, "yes" or "no." [3]

There were many such means of consulting the oracles in the ancient world, but all of them revolved around the principle that it was the choice between one of two answers. Tossing a coin or drawing the short stick are based upon the same principle. From the period of the New Kingdom in Egypt (1546-1085 B.C.) we have another example of the same procedure. The Egyptian peasant went to the falcon god Horus, whose temple was at Edfu. He asked his question so that the god could answer simply "yes" or "no." How the god answered has been discovered by archaeologists. A statue of the god, carved out of hard serpentine, has been recovered from that temple.[4] Through the bird-god's body a hole was drilled from the base to the beak. Another hole connected with the crown of the head. Apparently the purpose of these holes was that a hidden priest could manipulate a cord moving either beak or headdress. One

[2] *Ibid.*, p. 47; and G. A. Barton, *Archaeology and the Bible*, (7th ed. rev.; Philadelphia: American Sunday-School Union), 1937, p. 370.

[3] Williams, *op. cit.*, p. 80; W.O.E. Oesterley and T. H. Robinson, *Hebrew Religion: Its Origin and Development* (New York: The Macmillan Co., 1937), p. 166.

[4] Oriental Institute Museum, Egyptian Hall, Alcove E2, No. 10504.

movement of the beak could signify an affirmative answer; two such movements might indicate a negative response. This Egyptian system had at least the advantage that the intelligence of the priest could enter into the answer given in the name of the god.

The third method of legitimately discovering the will of the Deity was through the function of the prophet. Unfortunately for us the word "prophet" is used in our Bible to designate a variety of individuals and their special abilities. We have tried to catalogue them in our own minds by calling some of them false and others true prophets, but this is not altogether satisfactory. The fact is that some of the men to whom we believe this title most appropriately belongs refused themselves to be classified by it. Amos at Bethel was addressed as prophet; but he was quick to retort that he was neither a prophet, nor the son of a prophet (7:14 K.J.V.). He refused to be known as a professional prophet. This was because professional prophecy was far from the thing that Amos was trying to do. This confusion of functions and terminology has led to many misunderstandings concerning the true significance of the prophets.

The prophet still needs to be rescued from the unfortunate terminology and distorted ideas that have surrounded him and his work. The word "prophet" indicates literally what is the function of a prophet. It has two syllables: the prefix "pro" and a syllable "phet," which comes from a Greek verb meaning "to speak." A prophet is therefore one who speaks for, or on behalf of, God. He does not necessarily speak "pre," or ahead of time. Prophecy has been confused with prediction, but such confusion is made by those who have not studied the work of the prophets in relation to their own day. That which passes for "interpretation" of the prophets today is actually misrepresentation. They were only incidentally interested in prediction. To be sure, they did warn their countrymen that if they persisted in immoral conduct and if they trusted in political pacts rather than in God, the nation would inevitably find itself in political captivity. They certainly did not peer into the distant future and make predictions many hundreds of years in advance. For one thing they were too busy seeking moral reform for their own day to be concerned about generations unborn.

The prophets were impatient individuals, so impatient indeed that they had no sympathy for slow educational processes; they sought the way of immediate reformation and sometimes of revolution. They were calling men to immediate repentance, for they believed that the day of judgment was near. Sometimes they were far too impatient. They needed to discover that the "mills of God grind slowly, yet they grind exceedingly small." The words "Come now, and let us reason together" (Isa. 1:18) were strange upon a prophet's lips, and actually the prophet Isaiah put these words upon the lips of God; they were not his own. It is perhaps fortunate that the prophets were so impatient. They could not have lashed men's consciences so successfully had they been otherwise.

Many of the biblical writings have been sorely misunderstood because so many attempts have been made to use them as keys to history, particularly the contemporary scene. Two books which have been so treated are Daniel and the Revelation. The book of Daniel was written in the second century B.C. for the purpose of bringing encouragement to a people struggling for their very existence. The Jews had revolted against their political master, the Greeks. They had had severe provocation; and now revolt had become warfare, a religious war. The message of Daniel is clear: just as God brought us safely through the bitter experience of the Exile, so he will lead us today. The purposes of God cannot be thwarted by any political figure or power. Righteousness will triumph. These words, coming in the midst of a bitter struggle, must have brought much encouragement to the embattled Jews. They could not be defeated; God was on their side, for theirs was the cause of righteousness.

But there are those who insist that the message of Daniel is to reveal the events of the end of this age. They insist that it is being fulfilled in these days and that the end is very near. However, let us ask this question. Just what encouragement would have been brought to the Jews who were struggling for religious freedom if in effect the message of Daniel was: Cheer up! Everything will turn out all right. In the twentieth century, anno Domini, there will be a great world struggle between the United Nations and the Axis forces, but the United Nations will win! How those Jews would have been encouraged!

Similarly with the book of the Revelation. It was written by a man who was himself a political prisoner. He was careful to compose a message that would get through to the new Christian churches in their time of persecution. Of necessity he had to write cryptically; otherwise he would have been condemned to death, and his message could not have been delivered. His message of encouragement is similar to that of the book of Daniel, but he has some specific things to say about the persecutors of the early Church. He was quite sure that Caesar would die and that the purposes of God were eternal. But he could not announce bluntly the Caesar's death. He therefore put the Caesar's name into numerical value, totaling six hundred and sixty-six (or 606).

This number has provided a happy hunting ground for interpreters. The number of the beast has been discovered to fit an almost countless host. During the Protestant Reformation the reformers proved to their own satisfaction that the beast was the pope of Rome, but Roman Catholics quickly retaliated by proving that the number fitted Martin Luther. During the First World War it was Kaiser Wilhelm of Germany who was designated the beast. In World War II the number was applied to Hitler, Mussolini, and Hirohito in turn.

Typical was a chart which I examined a few years ago. It proved that Adolph Hitler was the "beast and his number is six hundred and sixty-six." The chart had put the letters of Hitler's name into corresponding Greek letters and given their numerical value. It was prepared to impress those who had no knowledge of Greek, for there were three mistakes which made it possible to arrive at the correct total. The mistakes were based on similarities in form between Greek and English letters, which, however, are not equivalent in sound. Surely interpretation of truth based upon purposely incorporated mistakes is suspect. Moreover, we raise the question, What encouragement would the persecuted Christian Church of the early second century have derived from the knowledge of what was to happen eighteen hundred years hence? Biblical messages were written for the immediate benefit of the people of that day.

We hasten to recognize, also, that the messages were of permanent significance, and the religious truths discovered in the experiences of the writers are as valid today as then. The prophets were concerned with bringing moral understanding to the people of their generation, not with writing cryptograms to entertain or befuddle sincere but mistaken individuals millenniums of years removed from their time.

The prophets were pioneers in religious thought. They were absolutely essential to the onward march of men on the trail of religious adventure and discovery. There is danger, as we view the development of various religious concepts and think in terms of the onward sweep of history, that we shall be betrayed into thinking that man was always progressing, that it was ever a forward-facing mass of marchers on the religious trail.

A detailed examination of history will quickly dispel these mirages of the imagination. There were times when men climbed to mountain heights that brought new ever-opening vistas of land to be possessed. There were times when men sank into the cesspools that are always to be found at the center of decadent civilization. There were many times when men turned back to the land that had already been possessed, to patterns of thought that were wholly familiar. They feared to break new trails, particularly if those trails would take them over rough terrain that can strain the heart and lungs of a man. They knew not what pitfalls lay beneath the surface or what vicious animals prowled beside the trail watchfully awaiting the moment when vigilance should be relaxed and weary wanderers could be taken as easy prey. Pioneers were needed to break religious trails; for only as such dared to break new trails and indicate the rich rewards that lay waiting on the new frontiers, could men be persuaded to break camp where life had been made comfortable.

Since one of the major functions of religion has been to bring certainty into life, men have shunned the unfamiliar in religious thought. They still want to be told what to believe, what is correct religious behavior, what the precise steps to salvation are. They do not want to think in religion, to apply to life the great principles that have been given to them. The more mechanical religious conduct and procedure can become, the greater the number of adherents to that particular brand of religion. That is why, when religion is left to an institution, it tends to become mere formality; and it declines and goes into stagnation and decay. This is not to say that the church as an institution cannot make progress in thought; it can. But that progressive thought comes only as individuals spearhead the attack, lead the way to new frontiers, and dare to challenge the authority of the old guard that is always more concerned about protecting the gains made by former generations than it is in making some gains for itself.

An orthodox position is alway one that can be validated by an appeal to history and to that extent is a position that has been discovered by generations now dead. The prophets and Jesus were not orthodox because they could appeal not to history but only to the validity of their own experiences. Generations had to pass before their positions were accepted as orthodox. It is always easier to defend an old position than it is to demonstrate the tenability of a new position. That is largely because the defenses have been handed on by tradition and one simply learns them by rote, but to take a new position means that the pioneer is without precedent. He must think for himself, and most men do not want to think. The reason that the prophets stand out by themselves, and in the judgment of history tower above their contemporaries, is because they dared to question old positions and to propose new principles. That took moral and intellectual courage.

How did these men arrive at their convictions, and what was it that gave them the courage of their convictions? Ever and again they announce their messages in the ringing and challenging words "Thus saith the Lord." What made them so sure? These three factors seem to have entered into the minds of each of the prophets whose words have been preserved to us:

First, the prophet had an overwhelming conviction that the old answers were inadequate. It was Jeremiah who saw that the old answer of nationalism was inadequate. Events were crowding each other so quickly that most men of his time must have felt dazed. He saw that the day was quickly coming when the nation would cease to be, and that the most that could be hoped for was that a remnant would somehow be saved which eventually might be a nucleus from which a new and purged people could spring. He saw religion had to be liberated from its ties to the nation; otherwise when the nation died, religion would be wiped out. A new answer was needed, and he found it in his concept of man's responsibility to God instead of to the nation.

Elijah and Hosea both knew, but for different reasons, that

the old answers of Baalism were inadequate. Elijah saw nothing in the claims of the followers of Baal for which he could not make a claim in behalf of his own Deity. Call it jealousy of competing religions or what you will, nevertheless Elijah was sure that the God he knew could perform all the things that others claimed for other religions; and as we have seen, this was a step in the direction of man's discovery of monotheism. Hosea was concerned from another point of view. He was convinced that the magical techniques of the Baal religion, and its philosophy that material prosperity was the great goal that man needed to seek, were conducive to moral decay and did not lead men to righteous living. Another answer needed to be found, and he was sure that he had found it in his message that the God of all men has an interest and a concern for those whom he has created.

It was Malachi who pleaded so eloquently for the establishment of ritual that was sincere, and he made his plea in a day when men believed it was essential that the liturgy be performed but were not concerned that it was no longer an instrument to make men conscious of God's presence and his power to bless. The ritual must be performed, for it was essential; but it mattered little how it was done or what was the attitude of the ministrants and congregation. Malachi knew that such mechanical performance was not instrumental in bringing the pouring out of God's blessing. He therefore proposed that men should put God and his claims first.

Not only did the prophets see the inadequacy of the old answers; but as they proposed substitutes, they dared to apply the ruthless test of logic. Theirs was not wishful thinking, nor can they be accused of voicing pious platitudes which would be pleasing to the crowds. Their messages would have made little impact upon their hearers and would quickly have been forgotten except for the logic of their positions. It was this logic that made men uneasy, and the attempts of challenged leaders to quiet the messages of these prophets indicates that they dared not risk a comparison of positions.

Amos' stinging criticism of the failure of religious and political leadership left the priest of Bethel quivering behind the platitude that the temple in Bethel was the king's sanctuary and therefore was not subject to the open criticism of free-lance

147

prophets. Amos let it be known that the people had been misled by false promises. Instead of great material prosperity and political supremacy being their lot in the day of the Lord, it was to be a day of judgment. Since they claimed to have been God's people and to have known the mind of God better than any other people, then said Amos, theirs was the greater moral responsibility, and the day of the Lord would be more intolerable for them than for any other people. It was this same logical thinking that led Amos to his discovery of the moral nature of God, for he knew not only that none but a moral God had the right to demand moral conduct from people, but that only a moral God could create a moral universe.

The message of Habakkuk differs from all others because in it the prophet dared to address to the Deity questions that arose from his logical thinking. He saw moral decay all about him, and he heard men say that God wasn't interested. Men could do what they wanted to, and there would be no moral consequences. In his meditation on this particular problem Habakkuk was at first satisfied with the answer that the onward march of the Neo-Babylonian army was God's answer. Punishment was coming after all. But as he continued to ponder, Habakkuk was less and less pleased with his conviction; for if the Neo-Babylonians were coming as an instrument in the hands of God for the punishment of Israel's sins, then what of the moral conduct of the Neo-Babylonians, who had far lower standards than Israel? And as he pondered, he became convinced that God was overlooking the conduct of the Neo-Babylonians temporarily because ultimately they would be entirely destroyed. In the light of the knowledge of that day this answer was quite logical. It would not entirely satisfy us now, for we have the added knowledge of the political movements of that day and of the personal ambitions that lay on either side. Yet perhaps there is a punishment, or at least consequence, that comes to nations who are immoral in their international relations.

Ezekiel not only followed in the footsteps of Jeremiah in teaching the need for men's acceptance of personal moral responsibility, but he saw the necessity for changing the institution so that it could minister to men who were struggling to change their lives, repent of their sins, and grasp this new opportunity that had been offered them. When the elders of the city came to him for advice (14:1 ff.), he knew that it was illogical for them to ask him for guidance in the name of the religion of Yahweh when indeed they were committed to idol worship. It was first necessary to repent, to put aside all apostasy, then to seek advice from a prophet of Yahweh. His clear thinking made his message of repentance clear-cut, and he refused to be turned aside by any attractive compromises with the elaborate religions of the prosperous Mesopotamian people. For him, as for prophets of other days, compromise was intellectual dishonesty; and that had no place in the thinking of the prophets.

They may have been mistaken at times, but the prophets thought as clearly as they knew how, and they refused to modify their positions either for personal gain or for the sake of personal safety. Most of them indeed were rejected in their own day, and it is the verdict of history not of their contemporaries that they were sincere and sound in their judgments.

There was another factor that entered into their experiences that gave a note of authority to their words, and this was their own religious experiences and their sense of companionship with the Divine. Whatever other impressions one may have from reading the words of the prophets, one cannot read them without the conviction that these men had a profound sense of the presence of God in their lives and the world in which they lived. Jeremiah may have rebelled at times that God was not treating him fairly, yet he never lost the sense of the nearness of God as Job did. Amos says of his experience, The Lord took me from behind the flock." These are not the beautiful phrasings of a poet who seeks to adorn his message. This is the stark reality of the prose of a prophet's life. He was under conviction to speak, and only the conviction that he was a messenger of God could have persuaded him to journey to Bethel and to confront priests and people alike with a message that was more condemnation than anything else. Isaiah was so certain that he was God's spokesman that he dared to challenge King Ahaz as the king checked the city's defenses and its water supply. Isaiah was so sure that he was voicing the truth that he dared to give his children names that were constant reminders to the people of Jerusalem of the messages that he had delivered. On another occasion he committed his writing to a clay tablet in good

Assyrian style, rolled its surface with a sealing roll so that its content could not be changed, and left the judgment to the future.

We may be disturbed by some of the anthropomorphisms with which the prophets described the Deity and his activities. It is difficult to tell at times whether they are describing literally their impressions or if they are using old phrases in poetical sense. Like many another individual they may have been overwhelmed at the task of putting into words the spiritual experiences that had been theirs. They use the brush of the artist to paint as graphically as they know how the rich joys they have experienced, and they trust the very intensity of their pictures will carry to their hearers the reality with which they have come to know God. A later day tried to spiritualize man's concept of God and to rid his vocabulary of crass imagery, but this very attempt in the postexilic period resulted in a transcendentalism that left God far removed from the world of men. He was active in nature, in history, and in contemporary events. It was this that spurred the prophets on to action in his behalf.

The prophets were not alike, and it would be futile to attempt to classify them by types. These men arrived at their messages in a variety of ways. God is a respecter of the differences in human personality. To Amos, God's word came as the prophet observed the social scene and carefully analyzed what he saw. To Hosea an understanding came through personal suffering. To Isaiah a great conviction came as he meditated for himself and for his people in the quiet of the Temple. Insight came to Jeremiah through his prayer life. And to Ezekiel the message came as he served as a priest in God's church. The prophets were never human stenographers taking divine dictation. They were deeply religious men who speak to us out of the depths of their experience. Religion cannot be dictated; it must be experienced. Only an intimate acquaintance with the individual characteristics of each of these men can give us an appreciation of why that particular individual must say, "Thus saith the Lord."

PART THREE

Men Who Blazed the Trail

11

Amos: Prophet of Moral Responsibility

◆

OCCASIONALLY THERE DID APPEAR AN INDIVIDUAL WHO WAS a rebel against the regular organization of things. Such an individual was Amos. He functioned as a prophet was expected to do, but he refused to be labeled as one. He prepared his messages in verse as was the custom of the prophet. He delivered those messages at the time of the great festival at Bethel, undoubtedly taking advantage of the regular opportunity that was granted to the prophets on such occasions. The message of Amos was and is disturbing, not because of delivery in loud tones, but because of its indictment of fundamental ills in a prosperous society. Here was a man who had thought long and carefully concerning the conditions he saw. His keenly analytical mind led him to convictions that are now recognized as being astute observations upon human nature. He was the kind of individual who has been responsible for putting conscience into religion.

Amos was born in the early part of the eighth century before Christ. The only town with which he is associated apart from Bethel is the little town of Tekoa, situated only six miles from Bethlehem and twelve miles from Jerusalem. Here he had the double occupation of tending sheep and caring for sycamore fig trees on the nearby slopes. The latter job quite probably involved hand pollination to secure necessary fertilization. This process was well known in Mesopotamia and must have been practiced to some extent in Palestine. The work of Amos took him to the Northern Kingdom to sell wool and perhaps figs. In his travels he became acquainted with the people of the Northern Kingdom, the conditions under which they lived, and the increasing disparity between rich and poor. He learned from other traders and from members of caravans the news of other nations. His messages include references to many peoples of the Near East, and it is quite apparent that he was an informed citizen.

We know all too little about this man. Our attempts at reconstruction of his life are feeble efforts, and sometimes our assumptions are unwarranted. Let us look at some of them. It has been claimed that Amos was an uneducated peasant having the typical reactions of a rustic as he came into awareness of the sophistication of city life. Many writers have believed that Amos was without education and that he has given us his message in some of the poorest Hebrew in existence. Since the careful work of William Rainey Harper the fine work of Amos has come to its proper place of recognition from a literary point of view.[1] It is undoubtedly true that Amos had very little formal education, but that is no reason for assuming that he remained an uneducated individual. His messages indicate three characteristics that are usually accepted as tests of the educated man. First, he was well acquainted with the traditions of his own people. Whether he had learned them from written sources or had become acquainted with them through the songs of the tribes around the campfires is unimportant. He drew his illustrations from the history of his people (5:25) and of surrounding peoples (9:2-8).

Second, Amos was a master of the language of his people. Hebrew is a language that is limited in vocabulary, having only about two thousand root words and a vocabulary of approximately ten thousand words as against one hundred thousand in Greek and a half million in English. Nevertheless, Amos made good use of the limited language at his disposal, for he used his words with precision. At times his phrases are freighted with sarcasm; at others they are piercing thrusts that send offenders screaming to cover. A final characteristic was combined with his skillful use of language to make his messages among the most

[1] *Amos and Hosea* in the *International Critical Commentary.*

outstanding ever given to the Hebrew people, and that was the ability and logic with which he organized his messages. He was not a man to shout out on the spur of the moment; but he gives evidence that having seen things that were displeasing in Bethel, he thought long and intensely before voicing his concern. If the methodology of Amos was followed by so-called modern prophets, they would be more worthy of the title "prophet."

Amos was not merely content with denouncing injustices as he saw them among politicians, religious leaders, and people alike. He denounced, but he proposed remedies. He also dared to face the culprits with his messages of condemnation; he did not seek the plaudits of men who would easily agree with him but who had no responsibility for changing existing conditions. If information concerning the culture in which one lives and the ability to express oneself logically and clearly are the marks of an educated man, then by all odds Amos was an educated man.

It has also been assumed that he was a poor man and that his cries on behalf of the poor are typical of that class. We have no way of discovering whether or not he was rich or poor. Nothing in the biblical record will help us at this point. He tended sheep, but whether he was the owner of a small flock or the shepherd of another man's flock, we do not know. It is also fair to note that righteous indignation concerning the injustices within society is not confined to the poor man. Men of wealth have been equally concerned in ancient and more recent days. The prophet of social justice is not necessarily one of the have-nots. We need to confess in the case of Amos that this is one of the points at which we have inadequate information.

A further false assumption has been that the prophets always appeared in times of political emergency and crisis. If by emergency and crisis we include moral conditions, then we may agree; but otherwise we shall be forced to disagree completely. During the youth of Amos and during the days of his prophetic activity, there were economic prosperity and political success in both the Northern and Southern kingdoms. In Judah, Amaziah was on the throne during the boyhood days of Amos. Amaziah had had difficulty in the early period of his reign but successfully established his power. Then came success, even to the extent of thoroughly subjugating the unruly Edomites. He was followed by Azariah, otherwise known as Uzziah; and the period of great prosperity was continued. At the same time there had been a mighty ruler in the Northern Kingdom of Israel, Jeroboam II. The exceedingly small amount of space given to this ruler by the compiler of the books of Kings is no indication of the worth of Jeroboam. Archaeological excavations have uncovered much evidence that this period was one of pronounced material prosperity. The strongest foreign power was Assyria, but this nation constituted no great threat until the coming of Tiglath-pileser III to the throne. If Tiglath-pileser came to Syria during the days of Amos, it must have been in the closing part of Amos' life; for there is reference to a threat but not to an attack by the Assyrian armies. The threat of political disaster was not the occasion of the appearance of Amos, but he was wholly concerned with the moral degeneracy of leaders and people. He condemned immoral leadership and just as thoroughly criticized false thinking in religion.

Palestine was a bridge between continents, and its people were normally buffer states between the controlling nations at either end of the bridge. In the middle of the eighth century the pressure was released. At neither end of the bridge was there enough power to cause difficulty for the people of Palestine. Great prosperity ensued, but with that prosperity there came unbridled desires and appetites. The merchants were making money, but there were crookedness and oppression. Amos cried:

> Hear this, you who trample upon the needy,
> And would bring the poor of the land to an end,
> Saying, "When will the new moon pass
> That we may sell grain,
> And the Sabbath that we may offer wheat for sale,"
> Making the ephah small and the price great,
> And falsifying the scales;
> Buying the poor for silver,
> And the needy in exchange for a pair of sandals,
> And selling the refuse of the grain.
>
> (8:4-6.)

Merchants had built themselves summer and winter houses (3:15), some of them of hewn stone, an expensive luxury.

The houses were elaborately furnished. Excavations by Harvard University indicate the extensive use of ivory inlay in decorating furniture and buildings.[2] Perhaps Amos knew of the house of ivory built by King Ahab (I Kings 22:39). He knew also the one-room mud-brick huts in which most of the people lived, houses which had wattle roofs and, like the poorly constructed house in the parable of Jesus, quickly succumbed to the effects of wind and rain. Amos knew of the abundance of meat, wine, and oil in the homes of the rich (6:3-6), but he knew too that much of that luxury was due to the unjust system of exacting fines from the poor. Note his biting words as he portrays conditions as he finds them:

Woe to them who are at ease in Zion,
And self-confident on the mount of Samaria;
Distinguished as the chief of the nations,
To whom the house of Israel resorts.

.   .   .   .

They who lie upon ivory couches,
And stretch themselves out upon divans;
And eat lambs from the flock,
And calves from the midst of the stall;
They who sing to the accompaniment of the lyre,
And compose songs for themselves like David;
They who drink chalices of wine,
And anoint themselves with the finest oils;
But they are not heart-sick over the ruin of Joseph.
Therefore they shall be the first of the exiles to
    go into exile,
And the shout of the revelers shall pass away.

(6:1-7.)

It was law in Israel that the poor man who gave his outer garment for a pledge when he borrowed money should be permitted to recover his garment at nightfall, for it was the only covering he had for his bed. In the experience of Amos he knew of families who went cold during the night while moneylenders and priests stretched themselves out upon the garments of the poor and drank wine purchased with fines levied upon this same poor

[2] G. A. Reisner, C. S. Fisher, D. G. Lyon, *Harvard Excavations at Samaria* (Cambridge, Mass.: Harvard University Press, 1924); and Olmstead, *op. cit.*, pp. 369 ff.

family, drinking that wine in the temple itself (2:8). Such lack of conscience Amos could not tolerate.

There was great mockery in religion, callous insincerity in religious practice, and shallow thinking among those who purported to be religious leaders. Upon them Amos let loose the full flood of his denunciation and biting invective. Too many of the leaders of the community expressed their religious interest through large offerings and legal tithes to the temple and not by putting moral principles at the heart of their businesses and lives (4:4-5). Amos insisted that this was insincerity, not true religion. The community made a legal recognition of the new moon and Sabbath holy days, but there were those who were irritated at the interruption it brought to their business operations. Apparently it was the same individuals who were crafty in their business transactions.

"Making the ephah small" may refer to the practice of some merchants who took advantage of the difference between the size of the Babylonian and the Phoenician weights and measures. These were the two established standards in the Near East at this time. The one system had weights heavier than the other system, and it was one of the tricks of the trade in that day to buy using one system and to sell using the other, and so make extra profit. Amos was pleading for a fair and trustworthy system of weights and measures. But he saw that the merchants who descended to such trickery nevertheless made legal observance of feast and fast days. This, too, he labeled for what it was, insincerity and not religion (8:5-7). He raised the question "What, then, does the day of the Lord mean to you?" There was strong nationalistic hope in that period for a day of the Lord which would bring material and political prosperity to the land of Palestine and liberate the people for all time from their foreign oppressors.[3] Amos insisted that if it was true that they as a nation had greater insight concerning the law of God, then greater was their moral responsibility and greater would be their punishment whenever a day of judgment should come. Logically he continued with the rhetorical question

[3] Cf. Chapter Seven, pp. 92 ff.

> Is not the day of the Lord darkness and not light,
> And blackness, with no brightness in it?

He saw that religion had become so much meaningless liturgy *had it been?* and was no longer instrumental in bringing men and God into right relationship. Because the religion of Israel had come too strongly under the influence of the religion of Baal, the techniques of sympathetic magic from the nature religion had now invaded the very precincts of Yahweh's temple. What had begun as dramatization of the love life of the gods, a drama enacted by the priests of the shrine and women devotees, had now descended to the place of being little else than a whole-sale practice of lust and licentiousness. Amos labeled it for what it was, immorality and adultery (2:7); but the community had put the approval of religion upon these practices. The prophet pleaded for a purification of religion, and he set up as a standard the old desert traditions.

> Was it sacrifices and offerings that you
> brought me
> In the wilderness for forty years, O house
> of Israel?
>
> (5:25.)

Now religion had become meaningless ceremonial, even to the place of creating idols of new gods to carry around in procession; but just as these idols were carried, "so I will carry you into exile beyond Damascus," was the message from the Lord (5:27). Amos saw clearly that any attempts on the part of man to please or placate the Deity through such elaborate but insincere and empty rites were doomed to failure. The great contrast is brought out clearly:

> I hate, I spurn your feasts,
> And I take no pleasure in your festal gatherings.
> Even though you offer me burnt-offerings,
> And your cereal-offerings, I will not accept them;
> And the thank-offerings of your fatted beasts I
> will not look upon.
> Take away from me the noise of your songs,
> And to the melody of your lyres I will not listen.

157

But let justice roll down like waters,
And righteousness like a perennial stream.
(5:21-24.)

There is little wonder that the message of Amos caused distress in the minds of the religious and political leaders, and that he was forbidden to continue his messages in the temple.

We have noted already that he was a religious rebel without benefit of ordination to religious office. It therefore was within the legal right of the priest Amaziah to deny him the right to speak in the temple at Bethel. Amos was not on the payroll of the king. He had no ecclesiastical office. Perhaps by his southern dialect he had indicated the section of the country from which he had come. Accordingly the priest Amaziah indicated that Amos would be much more likely to have a sympathetic hearing from people in Judah, who would delight in the downfall of their northern neighbors. The phrase "for this is the king's sanctuary, and the royal palace" (7:13) reminds us that the temples of that day were but little other than private chapels and open only occasionally if at all to the public. It indicates, too, that since the cost of the Bethel temple was underwritten by royal funds, the king's priest could deny the right of speech to any who were not officially appointed.

The words of Amos "I am no prophet, nor am I a member of a prophetic order" carry far more than a denunciation of that profession. They are a plea for the right of any man who has the message of God to be able to express himself. Not only is he saying that he seeks no remuneration for the delivery of his messages, but he insists that a man who has come to an understanding of the laws of God and religion is under divine compulsion to speak. Elsewhere in his message he says:

When the lion roars, who does not fear?
When the Lord God speaks, who will not prophesy?
(3:8.)

Amos brought a new definition to prophecy and a new understanding of its significance. By his actions and words he pleaded for a release of prophecy from all economic and political restraints. He was the first layman to appear upon the scene of history with a religious message. This is not to denounce all professional religious leaders, for it is becoming increasingly clear that the majority of the prophets had official and professional standing, but here is testimony that great religious insight is not confined to the professional leaders in religion. It is the basis of the conviction of most bodies in Protestantism that fundamental religious experience is the first requisite of the individual who may be chosen by the Church to be a religious leader. The minister of religion is not a priest who has been trained to techniques, practices, and dogmas of an institutionalized religion. He is a man who has found satisfaction in the religious way of life and is seeking so to share his experience with others that they may make the same discovery for themselves. With this viewpoint of religion Amos would find himself in complete agreement.

It has been suggested that Amos was destructive rather than constructive in his criticisms. To be sure, he saw fallacies within the systems of politics, business, and religion of the kingdom of Israel; and he did not hesitate to voice criticisms. It is true that his message was predominantly critical analysis, but had he nothing positive to propose? It is always dangerous to assume what was in a man's mind; but it is possible to see that Amos proceeded upon the following positive assumptions: first, he had a basic philosophy of life against which he tested the social and economic order; second, he was not content merely to criticize conditions as he found them, but he analyzed the contemporary scene and stated *why* things were wrong; third, he stated positively that it was essential to accept the leadership of God and implied that men should follow men only insofar as those men furnished leadership in accordance with the laws of God; fourth, he insisted that the moral law of God should be the controlling law in the life of men and of the nation of which they were a part; and fifth, he indicated that the test of any system of religion was the condition in which it permitted or caused men to live. All of these are positive, not negative.

It is essential that we recognize that the prophets were critics of a social and moral order, but it is more important to discover that their criticisms were always made in the light of a higher moral standard which they had discovered through religious thought and experience. Their's was a positive and challenging message because it called men to a standard of religious living that had not hitherto been known or accepted. It is the sober judgment of history that only as mankind has heard and heeded the challenges of such men as the prophets, has there come any improvement in the conditions under which men live.

12

Hosea: Prophet of Hungering Love

———————◆———————

HOSEA WAS THE ONLY PROPHET AMONG THOSE WHOSE WRITINGS
have been preserved for us who was a native of the Northern
Kingdom and also ministered to that kingdom. In point of time
his message was delivered within a few years of the time of
Amos. The message of Hosea was a natural complement and
also a necessary corrective to the sternness of the bitter denunciation by Amos. In the short time that had intervened since
the days of Amos, much had happened in the national and international scenes. A state of anarchy in Israel had resulted in
the rapid succession of four different kings. Good King Jeroboam
was succeeded by his son Zechariah, but after only six months'
reign he was murdered by Shallum. Shallum lasted only eight
days, when he too was killed. Menahem, his killer, now became
king and by political intrigue and murder remained in power.
The social and political instability of the period is reflected in
the writing of Hosea (7:3-4; 6:7-9; 4:2). He knew of murdered
kings and intriguing political parties. High officials were denounced by him as thieves (5:10).

On the international scene events had been moving with
rapidity also. The throne of Assyria had been seized by Tiglath-
pileser III. He was immediately successful in his campaign
against Babylon. Because of his military tactics his name became a synonym for cruelty. To the northwest of Assyria the
state of Haldea (Armenia) had become troublesome. Under
the leadership of their king, Sardurish, a confederacy had been
formed with North Syria which had resulted in cutting off
Assyria from its all-important metal supply.[1] It was essential
that Assyria re-establish its lines of communication to the
Mediterranean, but Tiglath-pileser knew well the danger of

———————

[1] The importance of controlling the metal supply was indicated by Professor
William C. Graham in his class lectures at the University of Chicago in 1932.

seeking to defeat the Haldeans in their mountain fastnesses. He therefore turned his attention to the coalition of North Syrian princes and after a three-year campaign was successful in taking the city of Arkad. By the year 738 all Syria was under the control of Tiglath-pileser. There was obvious threat to the kingdom of Israel, but Menahem averted disaster by paying tribute to the Assyrian monarch. Menahem's name is listed in the Assyrian records among those who paid such tribute. This policy of virtual vassalage was unpopular with the Israelites, but Menahem continued to pay. His successor, Pekahiah, pursued the same policy. All of this led to uneasiness among business and political leaders. To make things still more difficult for Israel, Judah had adopted a pro-Assyrian policy and therefore no longer felt impelled to pay tribute to Israel. There was a declining prosperity and increased taxation, and it is not without significance that Hosea nowhere mentions the poor. Rich and poor alike suffered from the reversal of circumstances that had come to their land.

In such difficult days the message of Hosea was highly significant. A careful examination of his message, however, convinces us that it was not the political crisis but the moral decline of the country that challenged him to activity. He refused to be betrayed into thinking that political emergency was responsible for the conditions he saw about him. On the contrary he saw that moral degeneracy was largely responsible for most of the conditions that prevailed in his country. He was convinced that his countrymen had turned from Yahwism to Baalism and that no change could come in the fortunes of the people until leaders and people had made a complete about-face in religious beliefs and policies. His message was so filled with the phraseology of the religion against which he fought that it has been difficult for us to understand many of his allusions. More recent studies of Near East culture and religion have thrown understanding into his words.

The book of Hosea divides itself quite readily into two major parts: chapters one to three, which deal with the personal experiences of Hosea; and chapters four to fourteen, which embody the larger message of Hosea. Among the many problems that have long plagued Old Testament scholars is that of the opening chapters (1-3) and their relation to the entire message of the book. It has long been felt that if we could reconstruct the experience through which Hosea went, then we should have some clue to the motivations of the prophet and perhaps an indication of the immediate incentives that led him to function as a prophet. Recent studies in the culture of the Hebrews and in that of their neighbors have made available some evidence not accessible to earlier interpreters, and this fact alone would necessitate a re-examination of the life and experience of Hosea.

The difficulties facing us may be summarized briefly under two main heads. First there are the problems that revolve around the discrepancies between chapters one and three. In general two main positions have been taken by various writers. Some have assumed that these chapters are variant accounts of the same experience and have sought by several means to bring the stories into harmony.[2] Others have settled the problem by deleting chapter three,[3] but there is no satisfactory linguistic evidence for dismissing either account.[4] The second group of problems concerns the evaluation of the story of the domestic difficulties of Hosea and Gomer. Was the experience fact or fancy? If it was an actual experience,[5] then we must face the problem as to whether or not it is realistically recorded, or whether Hosea is being reminiscent, interpreting this experience in the light of later results in his life. If it was fancy, then we must decide between vision and allegory.[6]

Some have dismissed the stories of Hosea's marriage all too lightly. They have given consideration to them as merely anecdotes on the life of Hosea or too indelicate for modern ears. Their means as an insight into the psychology of the prophet's life have been recognized, but the bearing of the stories of the marriage of Hosea upon the message of the succeeding chapter has not been logically traced. To be sure, there is no reference after chapter three to either the wife or the children.

[2] Cf. C. Steuernagel, R. Kittel, L. Gautier, T. H. Robinson, and O. Eissfeldt.
[3] Cf. K. Marti, W. R. Smith, P. Volz, P. Haupt, L. W. Batten, C. H. Toy, G. Hölscher, and H. G. May.
[4] Cf. Harper, *op. cit.*, pp. 207 ff.; and Pfeiffer, *op. cit.*, pp. 567 ff.
[5] Cf. J. M. P. Smith, *The Prophet and His Problems* (New York: Chas. Scribner's Sons, 1914), pp. 109-36.
[6] Cf. A. V. Van Hoonacker, H. Gressmann, E. Day, and C. H. Toy.

Again and again, however, there are references to the love of
Yahweh for Israel.

Let us look in turn at the problems of the dual stories in
chapters one and three, the relation between the marriage
stories and the message and call of Hosea, the peculiarities of the
marriage purchase in chapter three, the differing emphases in
chapters one and three, and finally a possible solution of the
apparent conflicts. We shall assume, until evidences shall cause
us to change opinion, that we have in these chapters evidences
of an actual experience in the life of Hosea. Most scholars agree
that chapters one and three are varying accounts of a single experience but disagree as to which account is the original story.
If the two stories could be harmonized, we might be one step
nearer to a solution; but there are outstanding variations which
cannot be lightly dismissed.[7] We must note that much that has
been written on this problem has been done largely from the
point of view of twentieth-century moral standards instead of
the prevailing social and moral conditions of the eighth century B.C. Then, too, many theories have been more concerned
with defending or in restoring the characters of Hosea, Gomer,
or Yahweh than with letting the facts speak for themselves.

Turning for a moment to the remainder of the book, what are
the outstanding points of emphasis? The prophecy is a message of doom, of condemnation of Israel for its sins; and it is
relieved only slightly with passages of hope and expectation.
Condemnation by Hosea is largely on two counts: first, a failure
of leaders and people to respond to the love and nurture of
Yahweh;[8] and second, wholesale acceptance of the low standards and the philosophy of the nature religion of Baal (2:2 ff.;
4:11 ff.; 8:4 ff.; 9:10; 10:1 ff.; 13:1 ff.). Herbert G. May has
correctly indicated that we can better understand the meaning
of the message of Hosea if we recognize that often he used the
phraseology of the Baal religion to express his own religious
message, a phraseology that was understood perfectly by his

---

[7] Pfeiffer, op. cit. p. 570, suggests that ch. 3 refers to a slave woman who is
rescued by Hosea to redeem her from her past life, and she is not the wife of
Hosea, nor is she to be identified with Gomer. This theory would leave ch. 3
without relation to the remainder of the book.

[8] See L. W. Batten, "Hosea's Message and Marriage," *Journal of Biblical Literature*, XLVIII (1929), 263.

hearers.[9] This peculiar phraseology is scattered throughout the prophet, in chapters one to three as well as in chapters four to fourteen. This phraseology provides a clue to an understanding of the marriage experience as well as to the religious message of the prophet.

In chapter one Gomer is named, and her occupation as a professional devotee (hierodule) in the temple of Baal is clearly indicated; however, the emphasis in chapter one is not upon the wife but entirely upon the children. The names of the children are of major importance.[10] There is nothing in the record to indicate that these children are not the children of Hosea. Attempts have been made to show that the children's names involve the idea of marital infidelity by Gomer, but this idea is not warranted by the biblical account. Hosea in common with other Hebrew prophets despised the Baal religion of Canaan. He fought more violently, however, than some of the others. By making a devotee of the temple the mother of his children, it gave him a powerful weapon with which to fight. He used Gomer, or rather the children borne by her, as a means of heaping ridicule upon the beliefs of the Baal religion. It was an accepted practice in those days to give to children born to the temple women special names that indicated the blessing of the Baal had been bestowed upon the child and the community. Hosea gave names to his children that taught the opposite, that Yahweh was displeased.[11] The name of the first child, Jezreel, meant "God sows"; but Hosea used the name to teach that "God will reap" (1:4-5). The second and third children were named *Lo-ruhamah* and *Lo-ammi*. If the two letters spelling *Lo* had been reversed, the names would have meant "Beloved of God" and "People of God," and the children would have had names already known. There are in fact four men in the Old Testament having the name *Ammi-el*. Hosea, by substituting the negative adjective for the noun "god," not only changed the accepted meaning of the children's names but made those names carry a message to the people of Israel. He

[9] "The Fertility Cult in Hosea," *American Journal of Semitic Languages*, XLVIII, 89 ff.

[10] See Batten, *op. cit.*, p. 266; and May, "The Names of Hosea's Children," *Journal of Biblical Literature*, LV (1936), 285 ff.

[11] This interpretation follows that of May with slight modifications.

must have been following a method of teaching commonly accepted in that day, for Isaiah followed exactly the same method (7:3; 8:3). These children, then, offer us another clue to the solution of the relationship between chapters one and three. The children are the center of the message of chapter one, and that message is that Israel is *not* the beloved of God *nor* the people of God.

The woman in chapter one was a devotee of a religion with which Hosea was not in sympathy. The children she bore were just as much a part of the religious cultus as she was. When Gomer was united with Hosea, it was not necessary for her to leave the temple life; and the record of chapter three indicates that she did not do so. From her point of view and that of her fellow worshipers she was a deeply religious woman.[12] The fact that licentiousness had grown out of the fundamental beliefs of Baalism stirred the prophets to action. Because the desires of men were gratified by a practice that bore religious approval, it became more difficult to fight it. It became increasingly difficult for the prophets to offset the inroads made by Baalism into the religious life of Israel.

As we turn to chapter three, we note that the entire emphasis of the opening verses is upon the woman and the love that Hosea had for her. There is no record of the name of the woman, nor is there any mention of the children. Hosea has been called the "prophet of love," [13] but W. C. Graham's designation of Hosea as the "prophet of unrequited love" [14] is a more faithful description. The application made in chapters four to fourteen was that just as Hosea's wife had been unresponsive to his love, so Israel had been guilty of failing to respond to the love of God.

The only apparent point of similarity between chapters one and three is the characterization of a woman guilty of harlotrous conduct. There is nothing in chapter three that indicates whether or not she had been previously married to Hosea, nor

[12] See Olmstead, *op. cit.,* pp. 437 ff.; and L. Waterman, "The Marriage of Hosea," *Journal of Biblical Literature,* XXXVII (1918), 193 ff.

[13] See A. C. Knudson, *The Beacon Lights of Prophecy* (New York: Methodist Book Concern, 1914), p. 89.

[14] *The Prophets and Israel's Culture* (University of Chicago Press, 1934), p. 62.

is anything said about her conduct after the purchase price had been paid. There were conditions placed upon her as she was bargained for. The purchase seems to have been a normal transaction known daily in that part of the world. The price was well within the known range of price levels in that day. There is the difficulty that Hosea should be under the necessity of paying a bride price for a woman who already belonged to him.[15] If under Hebrew law she had committed adultery, she would have been stoned to death. If she had been sold as a slave for any other reason, Hosea could still have claimed her providing he had paid her bride price at some earlier time. It is the troublesome phrase "Go, again" that has suggested the second-experience theory. But if we translate, "The Lord said to me again, 'Go,'" then part of our problem is resolved (3:1).

Other writers have seen difficulty in the use of personal pronouns. In chapter one the third personal pronoun is used, and in chapter three the account is given in the first person, but we have no right to expect that a speaker will always speak in the same person. His language will suit the mood and the occasion of the particular message. In any case the woman of chapter three is a devotee of the Baal religion, and there is no cogent reason why she may not be identified with Gomer of chapter one.

It is possible, therefore, to discover the following steps in the religious experience of the prophet Hosea. It was his hatred of the Baal religion that challenged him to become a prophet. To fight it, he united with a woman known to be a follower and devotee of that religion. As children come to this union, he gives them names that are a public denunciation of the religious teaching of Canaanite Baalism. He does it with the firm conviction that Yahweh is using him in this way to teach the people of Israel. No question of morality is involved. Marriages between such women and the Israelites occurred from day to day, and there is no doubt that Hosea's action was not questioned either by the followers of Baalism or even by the Israelites themselves. Apparently he paid no bride price at this time, and Gomer remained the property of the Baal temple. Now Hosea discovers that something has happened to him. Through the

---

[15] Harper, *op. cit.*, pp. 218-19; cf. Waterman, *op. cit.*, pp. 202-3.

years he has fallen deeply in love with this woman. She is no longer simply a means of producing children whose names shall be prophetic messages, but she is the mother and the beloved one. Already deeply in love it is not difficult for the prophet to hear the command "Go, love!" And this time it is "love," not "take." This time she must be completely his; but before she can be wholly redeemed from the temple life, he must pay to the temple her purchase price. She must undergo a period of probation, then she will be really his. Apparently she did not become his bride in love. There is a cry of anguish in this and in the succeeding chapters that betray his disappointment. The final result is that her unresponsiveness breaks the heart of Hosea. A second and deeper message of unrequited love arises from this situation. His message now is that Israel's attitude toward Yahweh has been that of a temple woman toward Baal, interested only in what gifts she can get and then going to the highest bidder. Yahweh desired more than that. He wanted the response of love to love. The message of Hosea was more than a statement that God loves; it insisted that God yearns for the answering love of man.

There is a threefold significance in the personal experience of the prophet Hosea as I have reconstructed it. First, we have an outstanding example of the complete devotion of a prophet to his understanding of the will of God in all of life's relationships. Nothing was held in reserve. Every possession and every relationship were used by the prophet to reveal the message of God. Second, the prophets, though oftentimes far ahead of their contemporaries in moral, religious, and social thinking, were nevertheless tied to the patterns of the day in which they lived. As we come to understand better the cultural patterns of the periods in which the prophets lived, we shall come closer to a thorough understanding of their messages. Finally, we have an indication that Hosea came the closest to a message of salvation of any man in the pre-exilic period. It has become the habit in some quarters automatically to classify as postexilic any message of hope. We therefore raise the question as to the motivation of the prophets unless it was that through their messages there could come a change in the thinking and the devotion of the people that should lead to the preservation of the nation. Hosea discovered his message through the depths of human suffering.

His experience might even be called vicarious suffering. The
great value to religion has been his message that man's hope
lies in his response to a God who first loves us. We shall not
hesitate to call Hosea the greatest of the pre-exilic prophets,
and it is not without significance that he who suffered greatly
transformed his suffering into a magnificent message.

The book of Hosea is significant not only because it is the
first prophetic message built upon an intimate personal experience as an illustration, but because throughout the book are
penetrating observations concerning the moral ills of that
period. Hosea teaches that knowledge, particularly knowledge
of God, is the key to life. He says:

> The Lord has a quarrel with the inhabitants of the land;
> Because there is no fidelity, no kindness, and no
> knowledge of God in the land.
> Cursing, lying, murder, theft, and adultery—
> They break out, and one crime follows hard upon
> another.
>
> .   .   .   .
>
> Because you have rejected knowledge,
> I will reject you from being my priest.
> Since you have forgotten the law of your God,
> I likewise will forget your children.
>
> (4:1-2, 6.)

It is worth noting that the words of Hosea which have been
quoted so often "A people without insight must come to ruin"
(4:14) have been used by educators and politicians without
recognition that the kind of knowledge of which Hosea spoke
was religious knowledge. Again he says:

> Let us know, let us press on to know the Lord;
> As soon as we seek him, we shall find him;
>
> .   .   .   .
>
> For I delight in piety, not sacrifice;
> And in the knowledge of God, rather than burnt-
> offerings.
>
> (6:3a, 6.)

Hosea was bitterly opposed to all attempts to find a solution
to Israel's political problems by seeking alliance with either

Egypt or Assyria. There is a constant refrain that Yahweh is God of the nations and that therefore Israel should turn to Yahweh and not to the nations for help:

> When Ephraim saw his sickness,
> And Judah his wound,
> Then Ephraim went to Assyria,
> And sent to the great king.
> But he is not able to heal you;
> Nor can he relieve you of your wound.
>
> (5:13.)

The prophet called the nation "a silly dove, without sense," that fluttered back and forth between Egypt and Assyria (7:11). Another description was to call it "a wild ass wandering by itself" (8:9). The threat confronting the nation was that Israel would be forced to eat unclean food if it journeyed for help to foreign nations, and there was also the danger that trust in political protection would finally result in political slavery (11:5-7).

Another failure discovered by the prophet was that of religion. Religion had failed because of poor religious leadership and because of wrong religious concepts. Both priest and prophet are charged with dereliction of duty. The people have stumbled in their conduct because of the stumbling of prophets and priests (4:4-6). Priests are accused of political intrigue:

> Gilead is a city of wrong-doers,
> Tracked with bloody footprints.
> Like troops of men lying in wait,
> So the priests hid themselves;
> On the way to Shechem they committed murder,
> They practiced vice.
>
> (6:8-9.)

So great has become the sin of the nation that

> The prophet is distracted,
> The man of the spirit is crazed.
> (9:7*b*).

This prophet apparently belonged to that group of Israelites who had no sympathy for the monarchy and believed that it was against the will of God that the nation had selected such leadership (8:4). He indicates his belief that God has destroyed some of their monarchs in order that the people might return their loyalty to him (13:10-11), but the people have retained the monarch and have rejected a theocracy. For the present king he has no respect, for he says of him:

> From the day he became king, the princes have
> made him sick with the heat of wine;
> Worthless men have made him drunk.
> For their heart glows like an oven, with their
> trickery;
> All night through their anger sleeps;
> In the morning it blazes like a flaming fire.
> They are all hot like an oven,
> And they devour their rulers.
> All their kings have fallen;
> There is no one among them who calls upon me.
>
> (7:5-7.)

The most outstanding picture in the book is the great contrast given in chapter eleven. It is a contrast between the anger of man and the anger of God, which has been tempered by his great love for man.

> When Israel was a child, I came to love him,
> And from Egypt I called him.
> The more I called them,
> The more they went away from me;
> They sacrificed to the Baals,
> And made offerings to idols.
> But it was I who taught Ephraim to walk;
> I took them up in my arms;
> But they did not know that I cared for them.
> With human lines I led them,
> With loving cords;
> And I became for them like him who lifts the yoke
> from their jaws;
> And I bent toward them and fed them.
>
> (11:1-4.)

There is a sudden change of mood in which God is pictured as giving up the nation to its inevitable punishment. But it does not last. After asserting that the people seek a change in God instead of themselves, God is nevertheless willing to change his attitude. The message continues:

> How can I give you up, O Ephraim!
> How surrender you, O Israel!
> How can I treat you like Admah!
> How make you like Zeboim!
> My mind turns against me;
> My sympathies also grow hot.
> I will not carry out my fierce anger;
> Nor will I again destroy Ephraim;
> For I am God and not man.
>
> (11:8-9.)

Hosea again has emphasized what he sought to teach by recounting his own bitter experience, that God yearns for the answering love of man, a message that comes close to agreement with the message of Jesus.

13

Isaiah: Prophet of the Majestic God

WHILE THE MESSAGE OF AMOS IS DRAMATIC AND POWERFUL, and that of Hosea is smooth and tender, Isaiah's message is characterized by beauty, dignity, and a frequent ironical note. Until it was recognized that far more had been collected under the title "Isaiah" than had been written by that prophet, it was difficult to make a true evaluation of his work. This gathering of material into one collection reflects a peculiar quirk in the thinking of a nation. To glorify one of its heroes, in this case Isaiah, the collection was made as large as possible; for the test of a man's literature was (at least in the minds of some) to be judged by its length and not by its content. There was some justification for the additions, for the extra chapters were thought to be in the spirit of Isaiah and the natural development of his earlier message. What is this added material? A comparison of chapters 36 to 39 with II Kings 18:13 to 20:19 will indicate that these chapters in Isaiah are not the words of Isaiah but history about Isaiah which has been repeated from the historical sources. Chapters 40 to 66 are clearly from the years at the close of the Exile and the early years of the postexilic period. Chapters 13 and 14, 24 to 27, and 33 to 35 have been recognized as apocalyptic and from a date much later than the days of Isaiah.[1] The recognition of a variety of authorship in the book of Isaiah has caused some real perplexity in the minds of many people. First, it has been felt that unless we knew precisely the authorship of a book or a part of a book, then it would loose validity and authority. The importance of any piece of biblical literature is dependent not upon the author but upon the truth that is there. We know almost nothing about any of the biblical writers; and we must constantly judge *them* by

---

[1] It may be that chapters 33 to 35 were originally introductory to chapters 40 to 66 but have become separated in later editions.

173

what they have written, not test the writing by men otherwise unknown. A second question has arisen. What happens to the reputation of Isaiah if so much of the book is denied to his authorship? In the first place, Isaiah needed no such efforts to magnify his importance as a prophet. He was already far greater than men had been able to realize; and had they but read his message intelligently, they would have realized that their tributes could not increase his religious stature. He already loomed so far above them that it was several centuries before they began to understand the significance of his message. Second, as has already been implied, there is testimony here to the importance which was attributed to him by later generations. This was real tribute, and it came from a nation that hitherto had largely rejected him. Finally, as we come to a clearer recognition of the material for which Isaiah was responsible, there appears a consistency of message and viewpoint that formerly was not apparent. Because of the differing viewpoints in the added chapters, it seemed that Isaiah was far from consistent. Now it is possible to understand clearly his strong insistence upon certain characteristics of God and upon man's failure to draw upon divine resources, a failure due to the great pride of man.

There is a curious blending of the bizarre and stateliness in Isaiah. Yet the two aspects of his conduct do not seem to contradict each other; rather there is a comingling of characteristics that results in the creating of one of the most amazing personalities in the Bible. On the one hand Isaiah has been associated with the upper classes, particularly the royal household. He has been called the "royal prophet." This designation has been given because according to Hebrew tradition he was of royal blood, being a cousin of the king himself. Then, too, one feels a majesty of personality as one reads his message. He was a noble figure whether he was related to the monarchy or not. Because of this recognition of his nobility of character and person he has been thought of as the "gentleman" of the prophets. Unfortunately this has prevented us from seeing the audacity of certain of his acts, which if properly understood do not detract from his nobility but do emphasize his complete devotion to his task as a prophet. Only a man of such magnificence of character could have done what Isaiah did on some occasions and still escape ridicule or bitter denunciation from his countrymen.

His unconventional conduct was the means of delivering his message, and his purpose was to draw attention to his message and not to himself. He believed in spectacular advertising, certainly not in hiding the light under a bushel. Let us look at some of his techniques of teaching.

There was the time when he went down the street singing a popular fertility song, the music and theme of which must have sounded strange upon the lips of a prophet of the Lord. It naturally attracted much attention, which was precisely the reason for such a startling procedure. Suddenly the prophet changed the words; and instead of singing a song of great expectation, he was singing a parody in which the vineyard was cursed instead of blessed. It was cursed because it produced wild grapes, an unnatural result of careful cultivation. One is reminded of the words of Jesus "No sound tree can bear bad fruit, and no poor tree can bear good fruit" (Matt. 7:18), and one wonders if perhaps Jesus had in mind the teachings of Isaiah (see Isa. 5:1-7).

On two occasions the prophet made spectacular use of his children, just as Hosea had done with his. The first is mentioned in chapter 7 when Isaiah went to challenge the king on the outskirts of the city of Jerusalem. King Ahaz had gone out to check the safety of the city's water supply, for he was afraid of siege by the neighboring nations to the north. Isaiah took with him his son named _Shear-jashub_, which means "a remnant will return." What a strange name for a child, either in the original or in translation. Those inquiring what the boy's name was must have been startled into asking, "And why is the boy named that?" It gave Isaiah the opportunity he sought, namely, the chance to give the significance with respect to the life of the nation. The child did not have a given name; he was labeled by a text for his father's messages. In chapter 8 there is a similar situation. This time a child was given the name which had already been inscribed upon a clay tablet, and his name was even worse than his brother's, for this one was labeled _Maher-shalal-hash-baz_, which means "speeding to the spoil, hastening to the prey." One wonders what they called him for short. The names given to the children were a part of the teaching program of the prophet and in fact stress the permanent and more important aspects of his teachings. The first name was a message for his own nation and indicated that whatever happened politically, a remnant would be preserved. The second was to teach that the political alliance of which the king and the people were afraid would quickly be destroyed. Such use by the prophet of his children is but one more piece of evidence which testifies to the complete consecration of the prophets. All that they were and all that they possessed belonged to the God whom they served. Nothing was held in reserve, and even the most intimate relationships and experiences of life became vehicles to carry the message of the Almighty.

We have already noted the prophet's use of a clay tablet (Isa. 8:1-2). This method of writing was undoubtedly of the form known from the Assyro-Babylonian lands. Because the signs have been made from triangular shapes pressed into clay, the writing has become known as "cuneiform." Materials have been recovered by the archaeologists which testify to the fact that this form of writing was one of the most used throughout the Near East despite the fact that only the most highly trained men could use it. The method of businessmen in the use of such tablets was to prepare the tablet of clay carefully. A professional writer usually was employed. After he had listed the items of the business transaction, then "reliable witnesses" (8:2) were asked to put their seal of approval upon the document. This consisted of rolling a cylinder, which had been more or less elaborately carved, across the surface of the written material. It did not make the writing illegible but did serve the purpose of making it impossible to introduce changes into the document. Isaiah's use of witnesses served, therefore, not to testify to what he had written but to prevent his words from being changed either by himself or by anyone else. The prophet was indicating that he was perfectly willing to let the future be the judge as to whether or not he was right in his message. This theme is again stressed later in the chapter when he says: "I will bind up my testimony, and seal my teaching in the heart of my disciples" (8:16). Further protection of clay records of business transactions was sometimes used. In important cases the tablet was placed in a clay "envelope" on the outside of which a summary of the contents was listed. This summary was likewise sealed by witnesses. It may be that Isaiah was using this same protection for his message upon the great

176

tablet, or it may be simply a figure of speech illustrating the safety with which he could give his message to his disciples. In any case we have evidence of Isaiah's knowledge of the cuneiform method of writing. Whether he could use the complicated Babylonian or Assyrian writing, or used a simplified alphabetic cuneiform invented some centuries earlier in North Syria, we have no way of knowing. His willingness to commit his message to writing and to have it sealed against alteration does indicate the sincerity and certainty with which he delivered his messages.

One other incident is of more than passing interest. In the scant garb of a prisoner of war Isaiah walked through the streets of Jerusalem. The modern equivalent would be to walk down the street clad only in one's underclothing. Prisoners of war in ancient days were virtually stripped of all clothing so as to heap shame and ridicule upon them. What was the purpose of Isaiah's unseemly conduct? It was occasioned by the unwise political trickery which he knew existed in Jerusalem. A movement had been started by Egypt in 712 B.C. to unite the Egyptians, Philistines, Judeans, Moabites, and Edomites in revolt against Sargon of Assyria. By 711 Egypt believed that the time for revolt had come. This revolt was centered about the Philistine city of Ashdod, but it was too slow getting into action. Swiftly Sargon and his cavalry advanced against that city and dealt the movement a smashing blow. The Egyptians ingratiated themselves with Assyria by surrendering the king of Ashdod to them. So quickly had the campaign moved that Hezekiah of Judah had not been able to participate, and thus Judah was spared not only the disgrace of defeat but from punishment at the hands of the Assyrians. Isaiah had no love for Egypt and thoroughly despised her political schemes. As a warning to King Hezekiah and to the pro-Egyptian political party in Jerusalem, he walked in the shame of a prisoner through the streets of Jerusalem. He signified that Egypt, that proud but dishonest political schemer, would also walk the prisoner's road of shame. If we are correct in assuming that the prophets used such techniques as a form of mimetic magic, it may well be that here Isaiah was bringing all the power of his office into play for the purpose of bringing upon Egypt the punishment which he believed she so definitely deserved. Isaiah constantly warned against Egypt as a political ally, not because he trusted Assyria more, but because he was convinced that since Judah had turned to Assyria for aid and had made political agreement with that country, Judah had no moral right to renege at the bidding of Egypt. Isaiah had a special name for Egypt, calling her "[Braggart] Sit-still" (30:7). He said:

> Woe to those who go down to Egypt for help,
> And rely on horses;
> Those who trust in chariots, because they are many,
> And in horsemen, because they are very numerous;
> But look not to the Holy One of Israel,
> Nor consult the Lord!
> Yet he is the wise one, and brings calamity,
> And does not recall his words.
> He will rise against the house of those who do evil,
> And against the helpers of those who work mischief.
> Now the Egyptians are men, and not God;
> And their horses are flesh, and not spirit.
> So, when the Lord stretches out his hand,
> The helper will stumble, and the helped one will fall;
> They will all of them perish together.
>
> (31:1-3.)

Isaiah's demonstrations against Egypt were spectacular, but it is unfair to accuse him of sensationalism. He did seek to arouse as much opposition as possible to Hezekiah's dependence upon the pro-Egyptian party, but he was seeking more than a break between Judah and Egypt. He was doing all within his power to bring about the downfall of Egypt, and he believed that this was possible because Yahweh was the Lord of history. He believed also that Egypt's destruction had already been determined in the mind of God; and though the techniques of the prophet may hasten the day of destruction, yet actually he was merely announcing the plan of Yahweh in respect to Egypt. When Egypt's destruction came, Isaiah did not want Judah to be punished with her. His conduct was frequently unconventional, but it was the demand of his office that necessitated such conduct. The beauty of his diction indicates that he was in all probability a man of refined sensibilities, and such an individual usually is incapable of the kind of conduct reported of Isaiah. Only his utter consecration as a prophet could have carried him through such acts, for they must have caused him real agonies of embarrassment. Surely the prophet needed and had courage as well as conviction.

We have already noted in part the occasions upon which Isaiah delivered his messages. A little fuller examination of the events in his lifetime will help us to appreciate the stirring times in which he lived and the significance of his message in those troublesome days. His ministry appears to have been longer than that of either Amos or Hosea and is usually thought to have lasted from his call about 737 B.C. until the close of the century. The year 701 marks the last known activity on the part of Isaiah, and from then on we are completely at a loss for information. While it is true that as a prophet he must have been constantly active, yet there are indications that he prepared special messages for specific situations, some of which we are able to identify.

It was the death of King Uzziah that first challenged him to prophetic activity. His call is recorded in chapter six. His next period of major activity came only a few years later when the kingdoms of Israel and Syria had entered into a political compact to take possession of Judah. So far had their preparations gone that a puppet king had already been chosen to replace Ahaz in Jerusalem. Tabeel had been nominated for this position, and his name was known to Isaiah (7:6-7). Either Isaiah had access to inside political information; or what is more probable in this case, the political intrigue was an open secret. Ahaz was naturally disturbed, but Isaiah brought him a message of encouragement. The famous sign of 7:13 ff. was given on this occasion, despite the fact that King Ahaz professed not to want any such favor from the Deity. A child was about to be born into the world, and the mother was undoubtedly known to both Isaiah and Ahaz. He would bear the symbolic name "God is with us" (Emmanuel); but just as significant as the child's name was the startling announcement by Isaiah, "Before the child knows enough to refuse the bad and choose the good, the land before whose two kings you stand in dread will be forsaken (7:15-17). This word of Isaiah was startlingly true, and within a very short space of time the Syro-Ephraimitic political entente was smashed. In another two years Isaiah was able to sing of the destruction of the city of Damascus, capital city of

179

Syria, an event which was remembered with startling clarity for many generations (ch. 17).

A dozen years later it was Israel's (Ephraim's) turn to suffer defeat, for in 721 B.C. Samaria was destroyed and with it the power of the Northern Kingdom. It did not mean the immediate annihilation of Israel, for it continued to plague Assyria for a number of years, but after the fall of Samaria the Northern Kingdom could not recover from this death blow to national sovereignty. There was a slow but sure end in sight, and the death rattles were already in its throat. This tragic end to the Northern Kingdom had its impression upon the Judeans, including the prophet Isaiah. Chapters 9 and 10 tell of impending disaster, and the latter part of chapter 5 is one of the most graphic pictures in all literature of the Assyrian hosts:

> So he will raise a signal to a nation afar,
> He will whistle for him at the end of the earth;
> And lo! speedily, swiftly will he come,
> None weary, none stumbling in his ranks;
> He will neither slumber nor sleep.
> No loin-girdle of his is loosed,
> No sandal-thong is snapped;
> His arrows are sharpened,
> His bows are all bent;
> His horses' hoofs are counted like flint,
> His wheels like the whirlwind.
> His roar is like that of a lioness,
> Like young lions will he roar and growl;
> He will seize the prey, and will carry it off,
> With none to deliver.
> He will growl over them on that day like the
> growling of the sea;
> And if one look to the earth, lo! darkness full
> of distress,
> The light is darkened in storm-clouds.
>
> (5:26-30.)

Isaiah uses the experience of Samaria to challenge Jerusalem and asks:

> Shall I not do to Jerusalem and its images,
> As I have done to Samaria and its idols?
>
> (10:11.)

180

We have already noted the revolt under Egypt in 711 B.C. and its place in the career of Isaiah. Scattered throughout his writings there are many references to his attitude toward Assyria as well as Egypt. He was thoroughly convinced that all the political powers were instruments in the hands of God. He expresses the clearest philosophy of history of any writer in the pre-exilic period. This becomes increasingly clear toward the end of his prophetic career when he is concerned with the threat of Assyria to the city of Jerusalem itself. Sargon II of Assyria was killed in battle in 705 B.C. and was succeeded by Sennacherib. The death of an Assyrian king in battle was the signal for widespread revolt throughout the empire, and Sennacherib spent the first two years making secure his own right to the throne and then moved out into the outlying provinces to put down the many revolts that had been occasioned. In 701 B.C. he besieged the city of Jerusalem. All its inhabitants were alarmed with the exception of Isaiah, who was confident that Yahweh would not let that city be taken. Hezekiah had already paid heavy indemnity to Sennacherib; but when that monarch demanded more, Hezekiah refused and prepared to stand siege. The king now sought advice from Isaiah. Had he heeded the earlier word of the prophet, he might have avoided this embarrassing difficulty. Nevertheless the prophet assured him that the Assyrian king would receive a rumor that would cause him to withdraw from the walls of Jerusalem (37:7). History records that Sennacherib did withdraw from the siege of Jerusalem, but nothing is known of the immediate cause of his withdrawal. The Hebrew writers credit an angel of the Lord with slaying the Assyrians. Herodotus tells of mice invading the camp and eating the bowstrings so that on the morrow the Assyrians were killed in battle. Modern writers have combined the records and indicate that bubonic plague was carried into the Assyrian camp by mice, and the ranks of the Assyrians were decimated. Hebrew and Assyrian records alike indicate that Sennacherib withdrew from Jerusalem.[2] Whatever the cause, the Hebrews listened with new respect to Isaiah the prophet.

The messages of Isaiah, though delivered in times of political

[2] Cf. Olmstead, *op. cit.*, p. 481; E. W. K. Mould, *Essentials of Bible History* (New York: Thos. Nelson & Sons, 1939), p. 255.

emergency, were concerned with far more than national expediency. Underlying all his teachings were important convictions concerning God and man. He began his prophetic activity with the conviction that Yahweh was king and the supreme ruler of all people. This conviction grew with the years, and he constantly emphasized the teaching that Yahweh is the Lord of history. Assyria and Egypt, together with lesser nations, were the servants of God himself. They were used to punish other nations, but they in turn would be destroyed or otherwise punished. This is why Isaiah insisted that Judah should put its trust in Yahweh and not in political treaties. God controls; and therefore, though Judah should not make political compacts with great powers, yet Judah would not be in danger, for was it not the nation of Yahweh? (see Isa. 5:26-30; 8:6-7; 7:18-20; 31:1-3; 30:1-5). Though Yahweh was the God in control of all nations, nevertheless he had a special love for Judah and was especially jealous of his own rights over Israel (see Isa. 1:8; 2:18-20; 8:19-20). His idea of God also included two other important aspects. First God is insistent upon real worship and not mechanical ritual. One of the clearest differentiations between true and false worship is given by Isaiah (1:10-17). Second, God has a profound ethical interest which is expressed in his concern for justice (1:21), for the poor (1:23; 3:14-15), in his denunciation of theft (1:23; 5:23), his denunciation of oppression (5:8), his insistence upon man's need of character (3:16, 26), and upon man's need for sobriety (5:11-12, 22).

The pride of man is the worst sin of which he is guilty, and it has become the great barrier which prevents him from obtaining aid from the Deity, said Isaiah. One result of the day of the Lord, said this prophet, will be the crushing of the pride of man and the exaltation of God. A graphic picture of political chaos which shall come as a result of man's pride is given:

Because they have grown haughty, the daughters of Zion,
And walk with outstretched necks, and with ogling eyes,
Mincing along as they walk, and jingling with their feet—
The Lord shall smite with a scab the scalps of
the daughters of Zion,
and the Lord shall lay bare their brow.

. . . .
Instead of perfume there shall be rottenness
And instead of a girdle, a rope;
Instead of curls, baldness,
And instead of a stately robe, a wrapping of sackcloth—
Branding instead of beauty.
Your men shall fall by the sword,
And your warriors in battle;
And the gates of Zion shall sorrow and sigh,
As she sits despoiled on the earth.
On that day shall seven women lay hold
On a single man,
Saying, "We will provide our own food,
And will buy our own clothes;
Only let us be called by your name—
Take away our disgrace."

(3:16-17, 24-4:1.)

The prophet has given a picture of the complete breakdown of
society. Battle has removed so many eligible men that the women
are willing to support themselves if only a man will give them
the right to be known as married, even though he has given
that right to as many as six other women. Pride has been the
cause, and the final result will be the crushing of man's pride.

One of the children's names had been designed to announce
another important phase of Isaiah's teachings, that of the preservation of a righteous remnant. He predicted that a day would
come when at least a portion of the nation would have learned
the great lesson of history and put its trust in God and not the
nations. Elsewhere he implied that this remnant would be com-
prised of those whom he had taught, perhaps his own disciples
(8:16-18). He had the conviction that a minority who had been
properly instructed was a sufficient guarantee that truth would
be preserved. He believed that there were some in the nation
who would learn truth from the experiences of the nation and
that this remnant would be preserved. He devoted much energy
to instructing the people so that they could not miss the lessons
of history, and he gathered about himself a number of disciples
perhaps for the twofold purpose of making sure that someone
would carry on his work of instruction and the preparation of
the remnant, and also of making sure that at least a small group

had been thoroughly indoctrinated. That his work was done well is indicated by the fact that the prophetic party was in all probability the direct result of this organization of his disciples. The prophetic party changed its membership constantly with the passing of years and during the reign of Manasseh was driven underground, yet it sprang to life again and may have been responsible for the succession of Josiah to the throne and perhaps was the prime mover behind the movement which finally produced the scroll of law, that charter of the Deuteronomic reform in 621 B.C.

The message of Isaiah was the first that Judah had had in which the preponderant note was monotheism. Amos and Hosea had delivered their messages to the Northern Kingdom. Isaiah portrayed such a great and magnificent power that the people of Judah should have responded more quickly to his message than did the people of Israel to the words of Amos and Hosea. Yet even in the days of Jeremiah the people had not yet learned the lesson which Isaiah had devoted himself to teach. A choir was singing the "Hallelujah Chorus" of Handel's *Messiah*. As they came to the words "The Lord God omnipotent reigneth. ... And he shall reign forever and ever," a young woman in the audience turned to her companion and sneered, "Huh! Does he?" There was question in the days of Israel, and there is question yet in the minds of many, concerning the efficacy of the power of God. Apparently only as nations and men go into Babylonian captivity are they enabled to discover for themselves the truth of the teaching of the Prophet of the Majestic God.

14

Jeremiah: Prophet of Prayer

———————◆———————

WHEN AMOS COMES FROM A PLACE OF COMPLETE OBSCURITY to become the most outstanding religious leader of his day, his life is worth careful examination. It has been the judgment of history that the life of Jeremiah was of such significance and that his life and teachings were worth careful examination. Small collections of his writings circulated among the captives in Babylonia and perhaps in Palestine. References are made to him in the books of Ezra (1:1), II Chronicles (35:25; 36:12-22), and Daniel (9:2). In the apocryphal literature also Jeremiah is accorded a place of honor, being referred to in the books II Maccabees (2:1-8) and Ecclesiasticus (49:6-7). Matthew in the New Testament seeks a number of times to indicate that events in the life of Jesus had been foretold by Jeremiah (2:17; 16:14; 27:9). Jeremiah has been important to Jew and Christian alike.

The book of Jeremiah is one of the most difficult of the prophetic books to understand, possibly because of its poor organization but more probably because of its literary history. The book itself tells us that Jeremiah originally delivered many of his messages orally, but that later they were committed to writing at the hand of Baruch, a scribe. This record was burned, then redictated; and at that time "many words of like nature were added to them" (36:32). From this it would appear that the words of Jeremiah as we have them recorded are an expanded form of what was originally said. Many attempts have been made to recover his exact words as distinct from the biographical material written by Baruch.

It is generally recognized that the present book includes (1) collections of genuine oracles, (2) biographical material by Baruch, and (3) scattered material from the Exile and later, not all of which is actually from the lips or pen of Jeremiah.

Because of the great amount of material that has been preserved for us, including biographical material, we have a better opportunity for a psychological study of the life of Jeremiah than perhaps any other prophet. Even so it is difficult to fill in the precise dates of his life. We can only approximate his birth about 650 B.C. We can only estimate that his work as a prophet began about the year 626 B.C. We have no historically trustworthy material concerning his death. There are traditions by Tertullian, Epiphanius, and Jerome that Jeremiah lost his life in Egypt by being stoned to death by the people he tried to serve as prophet. Still less is known about his friend and scribe Baruch. It is generally agreed that Baruch began to serve Jeremiah about 604 or 603 B.C., but even of this we cannot be sure.

Jeremiah appeared upon the scene during one of the most troublesome periods in Near-Eastern history, particularly as it affected the history of his own country, Judah. The Northern Kingdom of Israel had already disappeared from among the nations. Now the power of Assyria was on the decline. Egypt regained her independence in 645 and was once more a power with which to reckon. The Scythians invaded Philistia in 626 and were feared by all the nearby nations. It may have been the onward sweep of the Scythians that first stimulated Jeremiah to prophetic activity. In 612 the powerful Assyrian city of Nineveh fell, and with it the New Babylonian Empire came to dominate the Near East. In 605 the power of Assyria was finally crushed at the battle of Carchemish, and her political ally Egypt was defeated with her. This meant that Judah was now subject to the Neo-Babylonian rulers instead of to Egypt. There were strong political parties in Jerusalem, and they differed decidedly concerning national and international policies. Greatest among their differences was the problem of whether Judah should seek protection from Egypt, from Babylon, or should attempt political independence. Poor politics led to the death of King Josiah of Judah, to the attacks on Jerusalem, and finally to the two (possibly three) deportations in 597 and 586 (and 581?). Jerusalem and its Temple were destroyed, and Judah ceased to exist as a nation. Into such a period as this came Jeremiah. The responsibility upon religious leadership was great, but he measured up to that responsibility.

Even more important than his immediate suggestions concerning political policies were his discoveries that led to a fundamental change in religious thinking and practice. His emphasis upon personal moral responsibility was one of the monumental discoveries in religion. Jeremiah was one of that great group of men who in their communion with God found satisfaction and an understanding of life. Jeremiah, in giving so much of his personal reactions, gives us an opportunity to understand how the mind of the prophet functioned. We see the struggles through which he went before he had settled in his own mind just what his message could be.

Jeremiah has suffered from the label that has long been associated with him. On the basis of the reference in 9:1 he has been called the "weeping prophet." This designation does him grave injustice. His emotions run through the whole gamut of human experience. There are times when he screams out his denunciation of those responsible for the evil he sees about him. There are great moments of optimism when he sees the glorious future that awaits men as they build their lives upon the admonitions of the prophets. There are those tremendous moments when he shares with us the insights of religious conviction and the challenges that he hurls for men to know a personal responsibility to God. There are times also when he descends to invective and hatred, seeking the vengeance of God upon those who persecute him.

Jeremiah was under the conviction that he should not marry (16:2), for he could not ask any partner to share with him the persecution that would accompany his work, nor could he be responsible for bringing children into the evil world that he saw about him. All of this added to the loneliness of this great man. He was by nature a man who longed for companionship, but he found no answer to his need either in family or in other human relationships. His loneliness for human companionship may have led him to find satisfaction in his religious life. He became increasingly aware of a companionship that was possible with God.

Born at Anathoth of the priestly family of Hilkiah, he became a priest as was expected of him by his parents. His priestly training was always in the background of his thinking and action. Few except the priests in Jeremiah's day had the opportunity of formal education. Jeremiah was undoubtedly taught to read, to write, to minister at the altar, and possibly was given some acquaintance with the ancient records of his own and other people. Sometimes we find ourselves dismayed as we seek to discover whether some of his actions are due to his priestly or to his prophetic desires. Apparently they were never clear-cut in his own mind. It is needful for us to recognize that there never was as clear-cut distinction between priest and prophet as has sometimes been asserted. Many men who felt themselves under the conviction of God to speak his message of necessity became prophets. There was no other way for them to speak. They could not become priests, for they had not been born into the right family in Judaism. It is true, also, that priests undoubtedly had ways of making their convictions known to those who came to them for instruction.

What prompted Jeremiah to become a prophet? What was there that he could do as prophet that he could not do as priest? We still must recover much information concerning the work and purpose of the prophets before we arrive at a satisfactory understanding of this problem. Jeremiah announced his call to the prophecy, as most of the prophets did, by telling of a vision that he had seen. The challenge came at an early age, and after a struggle he assumed the responsibility. But throughout his life he stormed against the office of prophet (see 6:13; 5:31; 8:10b, 11; 14:13). His denunciation of the function of prophecy as practiced by his contemporaries was scathing. Part of his challenge to become a prophet seemed to stem from his observation that other men had failed themselves, their God, and their nation.

An incident of more than passing interest in the life of Jeremiah is recorded in the thirty-eighth chapter. He had been condemned by his countrymen as an appeaser. King Zedekiah assented to his conviction and punishment. He was imprisoned in a broken cistern, a cistern no longer able to hold water but still retaining the slime and accumulated silt of years. Left to die of starvation, he was finally rescued through the intervention of the Ethiopian Ebedmelech. His weakness and emaciation made it necessary for the ropes to be padded before they were passed under his armpits and he was pulled from the mire. The rapid telling of this story in but few lines has betrayed us into assuming that the action is likewise rapid. It is fair to assume that rescue was not immediate and that the padding of the ropes was necessitated by Jeremiah's weakened condition. Jeremiah's message to Zedekiah after his rescue was a repetition of the same message that had led to his imprisonment. Such action indicates bravery of the highest type.

Jeremiah seems to have been torn between conflicting purposes throughout the greater part of his life. The first chapter indicates indecision even at the time that he became conscious of a call to service. The conflict apparently was the subject of his first recorded prayer. He had learned to struggle with his problems in the consciousness of the presence of God.

The message given for Jeremiah to deliver was not an easy one. He had to begin with destruction, and only then could he proceed to construction. He seems to have been unwilling to recognize that it was first necessary "to root up and to pull down, to wreck and to ruin" (1:10). His desire was to build. He had of necessity to learn that the rotten superstructure that had been erected by his nation upon old foundations had to be ruthlessly destroyed. Then, and only then, could the magnificent structure already taking shape in his mind come into actual reality.

Another source of irritation in the life of Jeremiah was his conviction that God had failed him. It was God who had given him his message. It was God who had commissioned him to take the unwelcome message to the people, and it resulted in his persecution. He vainly imagined that God would protect him from such persecution because he was his messenger. Jeremiah had to discover that in carrying the challenge of a stern moral message the penalty often falls upon the messenger (20: 14-18).

It is worthy of note that as Jeremiah grew older, his outbursts became less frequent and less violent. In each of his recorded prayers it is apparent that for him prayer was indeed communion with God, a communion in which he could unburden himself of his heartache and despair.

Jeremiah seems to have followed the accepted method of the prophetic leaders by careful preparation of his messages, many of which are in exceptionally fine verse. His messages were delivered wherever he could obtain hearing; and when the precincts of the temple were closed to him, he moved to other public gathering places.

He sometimes discovered his messages through observance of everyday occurrences. The man in the market place or the potter at the wheel alike were the means of his coming to an understanding of God's message for mankind. He frequently used such incidents as the illustrations of his great messages.

As we have already noted, events moved rapidly in the life of Jeremiah and in the life of Judah in those days. When the Neo-Babylonian army moved against Jerusalem in 597 B.C., many leaders were taken captive into Babylon. The policy of the new empire was to divide and to conquer, to partition defeated enemies so that there could not be a consolidation of active nationalism. Friends of Jeremiah were transported to Babylon, but that did not remove them from his influence. Letters were written by him to those captives, and under his inspiration the captives learned the significance of monotheism (29:4 ff.). He urged them to pray to Yahweh on behalf of their captors and so improve their own situation. But the greater significance for them was that they discovered through experience that God was available in Babylon just as surely as in Palestine.

Then there came the time when official opinion was opposed to him, and he was forbidden to appear in public. This did not deter him; he dictated his messages to his servant Baruch, who in turn read them to the people. This was only partially successful for soon these messages were confiscated and destroyed, but it probably led to a more careful recording of the messages of Jeremiah than there would have been had he been free to deliver them orally (36:2 ff.).

There are indications, too, as we compare the various recensions of the book of Jeremiah that separate collections of the sayings of Jeremiah were circulated in Babylon and in Palestine. It is difficult to account for the wide divergences between the Greek and Hebrew texts apart from some such explanation.

Jeremiah began his career both as priest and as prophet in Anathoth. The immediate cause of his going to Jerusalem must have been the great reform of Josiah, which concentrated all religious and political power and leadership in Jerusalem. Later, when a kinsman died, Jeremiah asserted his rights and purchased the property of his kinsman at Anathoth, and used the purchase to demonstrate his faith in the future of the nation (11:18-23).

At Jerusalem he was slow in coming to recognition. He was of no consequence apparently at the time of the discovery of the scroll in the Temple, for it was taken for examination not to Jeremiah but to Huldah the prophetess (see II Kings 22:14). Later in his life he achieved a place of respect in the hearts of his countrymen. After the first deportation he remained as a religious leader in Jerusalem. Still later, when the Neo-Babylonian army destroyed so much of Jerusalem and took many others captive to Babylon, Jeremiah was allowed to remain in Jerusalem. When his countrymen wanted to flee for protection to Egypt, it was his counsel they sought. He was stern in his condemnation of Egypt and urged them to remain in Jerusalem, much as he disliked that city. So strong was his feeling against Egypt that he was persuaded to accompany the agitators only after he had been made their prisoner.

In Egypt he was at least their figurehead religious leader. Apparently his religious advice was taken seriously; for although 44:19 ff. indicates the great revolt in the minds of the women and the consent of their husbands, they felt that they needed to defend their refusal to follow the ways of Jeremiah. If the Elephantine papyri reflect the religious thinking of the Jews descended from Jeremiah's compatriots, then it may be said that Jeremiah failed; for there is no evidence in the papyri that monotheism or personal piety ever became basic in the thinking of the Jews of Egypt. Tradition affirms that Jeremiah died the death of a martyr, martyred because his religious leadership was unacceptable to his fellows. But wherever his place of residence, whether bond or free, he obeyed the dictates of his conscience and accepted the responsibility of being pastor of the people with whom he was associated.

There are indications that Jeremiah was in the habit of praying on behalf of people and perhaps in their homes as need necessitated. It is unimportant whether he considered this a priestly or a prophetic function. We usually consider it a priestly office, but what is the criterion? In 14:12 and 16:5 he is convinced that he shall no longer exercise this office, but the very prohibition indicates that such pastoral practice had been his.

His nature was such that he could easily sympathize with people. Perhaps the very loneliness of his bachelorhood led him to comfort, to counsel, and to console those with whom he came into contact.

The voicing of his conviction that he could no longer pray on behalf of the people is given in terms of the priestly office of prayer. The petitions are associated with the burnt offerings and the cereal offerings. In contrast to the office of priest in prayer the message of the prophet is branded false. But nowhere does Jeremiah indicate that prayer is no longer available in personal communion. Here may be the beginning of his realization that religion and nationalism must be divorced. That insight ultimately developed into a message of individual responsibility.

Jeremiah was accused by his contemporaries of a lack of patriotism and of treason. Even in a modern setting he would have difficulty in defending his utterances, and an unbiased jury could but admit that he advocated surrender to the enemy. His defense would rest upon his concern for individuals as opposed to the nation, and that is never adequate defense in a court-martial. But his sympathetic understanding of men and of the miseries that sprang from their exploitation by the politically ambitious left him no alternative.

The prophet may never have given thought to the question as to whether prayer is a priestly or a prophetic function. He knew from his training that there were certain responsibilities upon the priest, and these included petition on behalf of the congregation. The congregation in the thought of that day was the entire nation, not the immediate worshipers. Indeed it is doubtful if a congregation would be present at most of the sacrificial offerings. The great discovery of Jeremiah was that prayer could be an intensely personal thing, a communion between a man and his Creator. Prayer belonged to no office or profession. It was the privilege available to every man.[1] That is why Jeremiah dared dream of a day when no externals would be necessary for a man to be made aware of God. Every man would know God, not from the instruction of the priest or through the instrumentalities of a ritual, but from a personal awareness of divine nearness.

[1] Pfeiffer, *op. cit.*, p. 514.

The question of King Zedekiah "Is there any word from the Lord?" (37:17) attests the important place Jeremiah held in the mind of the king. It is true that the king received him secretly and that after the interview he was still a political prisoner, though in somewhat more favorable quarters. In spite of political opposition the king needed the spiritual guidance of Jeremiah. Zedekiah was the victim of conflict between political parties, and he had neither the power nor the courage to assert his authority. Had he done so, and had he followed the advice of Jeremiah, his own political fortunes and the political history of Judah may have been quite different.

The forty-second chapter gives an amazing insight concerning Jeremiah's use of prayer in the prophetic office. The citizens remaining in Jerusalem after its second attack by the Neo-Babylonian armies were afraid of further assaults and sought Jeremiah's advice regarding a proposed flight to Egypt. They requested him to pray to God for guidance in this matter. Their urgent requests and their fervent avowals that they would follow completely the instructions that he should give them a test to the fact that on previous occasions they had not been faithful in keeping their promises. The prophet promises to aid them, but he also indicates that he needs time for prayer. The phrase "at the end of ten days the word of the Lord came to Jeremiah" (42:7) strongly suggests that prayer was a serious matter for him. It need only be noted in passing that if the prophets had received their messages by dictation from God, then it is difficult to account for the ten-day waiting period. Jeremiah needed time for prayer, for it was through his prayer life that he arrived at his great messages and conclusions. He took the problems that faced him and his fellow men into his periods of meditation in the presence of God. Prayer for him was a real wrestling with difficulties. Prayer for him was not the lazy man's way out from responsibility. It was coming to grips with problems in the light of God's great purposes and laws. Nor was it merely meditation or cogitation. All of Jeremiah's recorded prayers indicate his awareness of the companionship and presence of the Divine. He felt his thought stimulated by that presence.

Jeremiah, more than any other prophet, gives us an insight as to the function of prayer as a source of the prophetic message. Prayer for the prophet was not a magical formula through which the Deity was forced to do the bidding of man but rather a means for man to bring his life into harmony with the great moral principles of God. As the prophets prayed concerning problems that had long faced men, their minds were stimulated by their very consciousness of God.

Strangely enough Jeremiah's leadership through prayer led to his tragic end. His message was rejected concerning the flight to Egypt; but when the Hebrews fled to Egypt, he was forced to accompany them. They wanted this man to be with them so that he could pray for them in times of necessity. Again his message was rejected. The men and women declared that when they had remained faithful to the nature religion, all had been well, but when they had followed the teachings of the prophets of Yahweh, fortune turned against them. Even King Josiah, who reformed Israel, had died a violent death; and the city which became the center of the great reform had been attacked twice and destroyed by invading armies. They failed to see, as perhaps did Jeremiah also, that Josiah's political ambitions had led to his death. But Jeremiah did see that which they had failed to recognize, that Jerusalem's downfall had come as a result of Hebrew political intrigue. Hebrew tradition believes that Jeremiah remained the political prisoner of these people and that finally he lost his life through the very people who had commandeered him to pray for them.

Jeremiah's prayer life led him to a number of significant discoveries in religious philosophy. As he viewed the centralization of power and leadership in Jerusalem with their resulting pomp and ceremonial, he realized that outward religious acts may aid the meditation of the worshiper but are more often substituted for religious conviction and moral living. He dreamed of the day when man would be so at home with his Creator that out of the quiet of his own heart he could commune. There would be no need of form or ceremonial, of symbol or shrine. Each man would be a friend of God, and there would be no need of the mediating office of priest.

Jeremiah recognized, too, that religion must be the daily living of a man in accordance with the principles of God. As long as the Temple and the priesthood remained, Jeremiah saw the chief expression of the religious life would in all probability be observance of ceremonial. That is why he insisted that man needed not the law of Moses inscribed on tables of stone, nor the law of the Great Reform written upon papyrus, but a new law of God inscribed upon the very heart of the individual.

The impending fall of the nation was apparent to Jeremiah, and he dared to wrestle with the question of the results of that event upon the religious convictions of men. It was commonly believed in that day that each nation had its god or gods. It was likewise believed that in battle each nation was led by its own deity and that in defeat the god, as well as the nation, suffered shame. Jeremiah was aware that the Hebrews needed to learn that here was but one God who controlled all nations, and further, that the reputation of God is not dependent upon the political fortunes of any people. To the people still in Jerusalem he affirmed that though the enemy should become their masters, yet religion would not go down to defeat, that God was using the enemy for his own particular purposes.

The early days of the political and religious reform under Josiah were hailed with delight. Evidences of Baalism were uprooted, and Yahwism was made the supreme religion of the Hebrews. The prophetic party had completely won their way. Josiah was king at their instigation, he had been carefully coached so that he was favorable to Yahwism, and now the new law (bearing unmistakable marks of prophetic influence) had been found and enforced. At the outset Jeremiah seems to have joined the chorus of praise; but when he saw the results of centralization of political and religious power in Jerusalem, he raised his voice in protest. Above all he saw that a religion of the book, whether written on tables of stone or upon a scroll of papyrus, would not answer the needs of men. It would lead to stagnation. Religion must be something that is vitally alive in principles that are inscribed upon the minds of men. Jeremiah therefore announced a "new covenant" written by God upon the hearts of men. So significant were the words of Jeremiah that they were used by Jesus and Paul, and through them have been given designation to the two divisions of our Bible, the Old and New Covenants or Testaments. Again his emphasis is upon the individual and not the nation with whom former covenants had been made. More important, he affirmed by this teaching that the law of God must be discovered by each man in personal communion and prayer.

The hope that is implicit throughout the message of Jeremiah is not for the nation except as the nation is composed of individuals (see 30:18 ff.; 31:17). The denunciation of nations and men by Jeremiah is intensely severe, but behind his message of doom is the conviction that there will be a day of building and planting, that the day of destruction will not always prevail. Hope is in God, but God will work through men as individuals. The great dream of the prophet is men whose emotions and intellects have been inscribed with the law of their God, and men whose minds could know the divine touch through the function of prayer. He desired for others what he himself had discovered, prayer and communion at the heart of religion and the source of moral integrity and strength.

Other prophets undoubtedly arrived at their convictions through the function of prayer, but none takes us so intimately into his confidence as does Jeremiah. Jeremiah has left for us not only his conclusions but the experiences through which he passed on his way to those conclusions. It is possible that when he confided to Baruch the burden of his intimate prayers, he had no intention that these prayers should be paraded before men. Baruch has been accused of having low intelligence and of not knowing what should be recorded and what should be discreetly hidden from the public gaze. But whether these prayers come to us through the misjudgment or the insight of Baruch, we are grateful; for through them we have an understanding of the intimate relationship between prayer and the function of prophecy that otherwise we may not have had. Prayer and prophecy take on a new significance because Jeremiah demonstrated the dependence of prophecy upon prayer.

15

Ezekiel: Prophet of God's Kingdom

————————◆————————

THE BOOK OF EZEKIEL HAS BEEN A GREAT CENTER OF DEBATE, first among the Jews and now among the Christians. There are a number of reasons for this, for the discussions have revolved around the questions of authorship, date of writing, significance and orthodoxy of the message, and whether or not the book should be included in the canon of Scripture. The book was included by the Jews among the accepted writings of the prophets and later by Christians into the Bible as one of the major prophets. Thus one of the questions has been settled, but others are still being debated. Authorship was attributed by the early Jews to "men of the Great Assembly," [1] but the majority of Bible students are agreed that the book is the work of a priest who lived in the time of the Babylonian exile.[2] Josephus states that Ezekiel was a boy taken into captivity at the time of the first deportation.[3] His life is shrouded in obscurity, and we have no information concerning its length or when and where his death occurred. Pseudo-Epiphanius tells of his martyrdom at the hands of a Hebrew whom he had rebuked for idolatry.[4] Despite the controversies that have raged around this man and his writing, he has been important from a literary and from a religious point of view. Much of the debate has been occasioned because this prophet dared to say something new, and to say it in a type of writing that had not been known among the Jews before his day. The rabbis objected to this book on the grounds that it differed from the accepted law of Moses and that its opening visions would entice men into theosophical

[1] See *Babylonian Talmud,* Baba Bathra, I, 14*b*, 15.
[2] Irwin, *The Problem of Ezekiel* (University of Chicago Press, 1943).
[3] *Antiquities* X. Vi. Cf. *Abingdon Bible Commentary,* pp. 714-45.
[4] F. C. Eiselen, *Prophecy and the Prophets in Their Historical Relations* (New York: Methodist Book Concern, 1909).

speculation.[5] Nevertheless it has become traditional to think of Ezekiel as the "father of Judaism." Whether the title is historically justified may be debated, but it is at least a tribute to the importance of this man in the history of Hebrew religion.

Ezekiel tells us that he was a son of Buzi and that he was a priest. He therefore belonged to a priestly family, possibly of Zadokite descent. He was married; and one of the most touching passages in the book is concerned with the death of his wife, whom he calls the delight of his eyes (24:15-27). No children are mentioned. The visions of Ezekiel have been studied from the point of view of the physical and psychological health of the prophet, but there is no unanimity of opinion concerning either his physical well-being or his mental balance. A recent psychological study definitely labels Ezekiel a "true psychotic capable of great religious insight" and exhibiting abnormalities consistent with paranoid schizophrenia and suffering from "narcissistic-masochistic conflict," "schizophrenic withdrawal," and "delusions of persecution and grandeur." [6]

Much difficulty arises from the failure of readers to recognize that in the book of Ezekiel we are dealing with literature that was designed as a written document, and that many of the experiences recorded are not literal physical experiences, but the writer has taken advantage of certain literary devices. For example, the prophet speaks of being "brought . . . in visions of God to Jerusalem" (8:3). He explains that he was lifted by the hair of his head and so transported to his destination. In the information that follows there is nothing that indicates his reception of any new information, for everything that he describes was known in the Temple environ before the days of the first deportation. Yet on the basis of Freudian psychology this vision may be given abnormal sexual connotations. As a matter of fact, as more information comes to us concerning the Assyro-Babylonian culture in which Ezekiel lived, it has been discovered that the visions of Ezekiel are more readily explained from cultural background than by abnormal psychology.

We shall need the help of the psychologist and also that of

[5] W. R. Smith, *The Old Testament in the Jewish Church* (New York: The Macmillan Co., 1912), pp. 149-87; Torrey, *Pseudo-Ezekiel and the Original Prophecy* (New Haven, Conn.: Yale University Press, 1930), pp. 15-16.

[6] Broome, "Ezekiel's Abnormal Personality," *Journal of Biblical Literature,* Sept., 1946, pp. 277-92.

the historian to understand this or any other prophet, and we welcome any light that can be thrown upon our subject, but the use of the one to the exclusion of the other will result in nothing but distorted pictures, and we have all too many of those already. It is our conviction that while there are some phases of the life and teaching of Ezekiel that are obscure, yet it is possible to recover the main essential of this teaching by proceeding upon the assumption that he was a normal individual who arrived at his religious conviction through normal religious experiences. Any other interpretation necessarily makes the reception of religious insight an abnormal procedure instead of the result of normal cognition.

Because of the many visions in the book, and because of the description of the overthrow of Gog and Magog, the book of Ezekiel has been called apocalyptic. Visions, however, were referred to constantly by the prophets from the days of Amos down to the time of Jeremiah and Ezekiel. It is to be noted, moreover, in connection with the conflict between Yahweh and Magog that though it results in the overthrow of evil and the vindication of Yahweh, yet it is not a cataclysmic end of the world and the beginning of a new age which is so characteristic of the apocalypse. After Israel has been brought from the Exile and restored to the land of Palestine, there is the final overthrow of her political enemy; but otherwise the picture shows not the slightest similarity to the apocalyptic pattern. Ezekiel remained true to the methods and philosophy of the prophets and did not retreat to pessimism and crisis theology.

Many phrases are caught up from the words of Ezekiel by later writers. This was inevitable because so many of his phrases are either of obscure meaning or lend themselves admirably to expansion of interpretation. Unfortunately the borrowers did Ezekiel a disservice for the reason that their use of the phrases differed decidedly from the original significance; and since so many of the borrowers belonged in the apocalyptic group, this same association has been made with respect to Ezekiel. The usual literary sequence in the Bible is as follows: the writer of Daniel borrowed from Ezekiel, and Daniel in turn was borrowed by the writer of the Revelation. Such phrases as "touch no one on whom is the mark" (9:6) ; the "cherubim" (10:14 et al.) ; "my four deadly judgments—sword, famine, wild beasts, and pestilence" (14:21); "will I cause a horn to sprout" (29:21); and many others were used by later writers and curiously twisted from their original context and meaning. Ezekiel is largely responsible for a new use of allegory in the literature of Israel; and as the years pass, this usage increases. But it should be noted that whereas Ezekiel uses many of them as simple illustrations, the later practice was to make them carry profound metaphorical meanings, the significance of which only the initiated knew.

Ezekiel has been charged with being inconsistent at many points, particularly in that some of his messages are denunciatory and others are conciliatory. In the first group he speaks of the coming doom of the nation and the fall of the city of Jerusalem; in the latter he indicates that there is a coming day of hope and restoration. It is needful to remember that his messages were delivered over a period of many years. A careful correlation of his messages with historical events will reveal that most of his messages of condemnation were delivered between 592 and 586 B.C. There were many optimists even among those who had been sent to Babylon with the first deportation who felt that nothing worse could happen to the city of Jerusalem. Ezekiel was insistent that there would be a full and complete destruction of their capital city.

After the city had fallen, his message changed to one of encouragement. The punishment had now been fully meted out to the nation, and the day of restoration was not too far distant. There is more evidence of literary organization in the book of Ezekiel than most other prophecies, and it is in respect to his message of doom and hope that this is most clear. After the opening chapters, which deal with his call to prophecy, the next chapters (3:16 to 24:27) are pictures of judgment. Beginning with chapter twenty-five, the book is concerned with Yahweh's vindication and the restoration of Israel. After the nations have received warning of their coming destruction and with it the restoration of the reputation of the God of Israel, there comes the news of the final fall of Jerusalem (33:21 ff.); and quickly the prophet moves on to a picture of the restoration of the nation. The constitution for a theocratic utopia (chapters 40 to 48) forms a natural conclusion whether this section is from the hand of the prophet or the skillful addition of a later editor. The change from messages of condemnation to messages of hope and reconstruction as circumstances necessitated indicate the responsiveness of the mind of Ezekiel to the needs of those whom he tried to serve.

Ezekiel did not confine himself to one technique of teaching, and this we need to recognize most clearly. However, we should also recognize that there has been preserved for us only the prepared written document, even though these writings include descriptions of other procedures used by the prophet. He was among the first to avail himself of the power of the written word; but he continued to speak in public, to use mimetic magic to induce certain results among men and nations, and to deliver oracles. He used a clay tablet and traced upon it an outline of the city of Jerusalem. Then he proceeded to lay siege to this picture of the city (4:1 ff.). Was he illustrating a message that he was delivering? It is more likely that he was using magic to induce the fall of the city which he believed to be doomed. When the city fell, it is quite likely that his reputation was considerably enhanced.

With graphic description Ezekiel tells of Israel's selection by Yahweh, a story that is decidedly at variance with the later traditional accounts of Israel's origin and relationship to God. Ezekiel says that Jerusalem is the result of intermarriage of Amorites and Hittites, a description which comes decidedly closer to the findings of the anthropologists than does the postexilic claim of purity of race. The hooked nose of the Jew is not Jewish except as that dominant characteristic was derived from the Hittites and has remained with the descendants of that mating of Hittite and Amorite. The birth of the child is described, and the picture is far from attractive. The newborn child has neither the benefit of attendance at birth, the cleansing by water in a settled community, nor even the crude treatment with salt that is given to the child born in the desert. God took pity upon the child, only to have the child as she came to maturity turn against her benefactor and turn to more lucrative sources. This allegory of the faithless wife had been used by earlier writers, but none surpasses Ezekiel in descriptive ability. To an Israelite the parallel drawn between the faithless wife and the unfaithful nation must have been obnoxious. It must be confessed that Ezekiel is not delicate in his treatment, but he was dealing with a problem that demanded harsh treatment.

There were those among the captives who looked forward to the day of political liberation and the re-establishment of the Hebrews as an independent nation in Palestine. There were those who were content to stay in Babylonia, for they had made a satisfactory adjustment to their new environment. Some of these forgot their fathers' religion and accepted that of Babylon, while others maintained the folkways and the religious practices of their ancestors. But the group that has been of most significance in the Hebrew-Christian tradition was a small number of individuals who became convinced that any contribution by by the Hebrews would have to be in the field of religion and not of politics. The Great Unknown Prophet of the Exile developed this viewpoint to include the principle of vicarious suffering, but the origin of this belief that the Hebrews had a privilege to serve humanity must have been stimulated in a large degree by the teachings of Ezekiel.

The priestly training of Ezekiel is apparent at several places in his message. There is first of all the use of elaborate and varied terminology, particularly with respect to the Deity. He uses a number of descriptions and names for God.[7] We note in the next place that he everywhere evidences sympathy for the work of the priests. We have already discovered that feuding between priests and prophets was not traditional, yet when necessary a prophet does thoroughly denounce those priests who have failed to respond to the responsibilities of their office. In the book of Ezekiel there is no such castigation of the priests. It is also clear throughout the message that while change should come to the individual as a result of the teaching of the prophet, nevertheless forgiveness is to be sought from God through the mediation of the priest. Detailed instructions are given concerning the purification obligations. Finally in this connection it is to be observed that the priest is the most important individual in the final picture of utopia.

It is impossible to discover whether Ezekiel functioned primarily as priest or as prophet. He seems to have been an important individual in the thinking of his companions in

[7] Such usage of names for the Deity was not practiced in postexilic times, a factor to be considered in dating the book of Ezekiel.

captivity. We have already noted that priests and prophets had specific places of responsibility in religion, each complementary to the other. Nevertheless, the conditions of the Babylonian exile were such that the regular duties of the priests were considerably curtailed. There was no altar and probably no sacrifices to be offered. Inevitably there was more stress placed upon the ministrations of the prophet, who was considered to be an expert in oracle and in prayer. Those taken into captivity were the leaders in the Jerusalem community; and though no attention was given by their captors to their family background or training, nevertheless it is a fair assumption that these captives were from the better homes and had had the best training and education.

It is altogether likely that the Hebrews taken into captivity were those who would be most receptive to new ideas.[8] There was therefore danger that the Hebrew religion would die during the Exile, for the Hebrews were surrounded by new patterns of religious conduct and new religious concepts that must have seemed attractive to many. It is a testimony to the wholesome guidance of Hebrew religious leaders that there came from the Exile a group of Jews with deepened and enlarged religious principles. Among those religious leaders we must number Ezekiel. Political defeat could result in destruction of faith and religion, or under wise leadership the people could find their way to new and better understanding of God and the essence of religion. Ezekiel, like Jeremiah, believed that the individual was the basic unit in religion. During the Exile the Temple was far removed from the captives, and religion necessarily took on other forms than those centering around the Temple. In the postexilic period the synagogue came quickly to development, and the Temple never again held the place it once had had, that of being the only official place for the performance of religious rites. The Exile and the synagogue placed emphasis upon religion as the servant of man and not man as the servant of an institution, as he had been in connection with temple ceremonials. This was in complete agreement with the teachings of Ezekiel and perhaps the result of them.

In common with Isaiah, Ezekiel believed that God was the

[8] Smith, *The Prophet and His Problems*, p. 193.

great moving power of history. The nations were used by Yahweh to punish the nation Judah. God is a mighty power, but one feels sometimes that the picture of the "God of might" is overdrawn and leaves one with the feeling that God wields immoral strength. Ezekiel likewise gives the impression that the Deity is far more concerned with his own reputation than with the well-being of man or even justice toward men and nations. The phrase "for my name's sake" in the sense of reputation is used frequently. Ezekiel announces quite frankly that the nation can be delivered from exile, not because of any merit of the nation or compassion of the Deity, but in order that the nations would know that God *could* do such a thing:

"And you shall know that I am the Lord, when I have dealt with you for my name's sake, and not in accordance with your evil ways and your corrupt doings, O house of Israel," is the oracle of the Lord. (20:44.)

Yet in contrast there is the tender message of God the shepherd:

For thus says the Lord God: "Behold, here am I and I will seek and search for my flock. As a shepherd searches for his flock on a day of whirlwind, when his sheep are scattered, so will I search for my flock, and rescue them from all the places to which they have been scattered on the day of clouds and thick darkness. . . . I will seek out the lost, I will bring back the strayed, I will bind up the wounded, I will strengthen the sick; and I will watch over the fat and strong ones, tending them rightly." (34:11-12, 16.)

There is likewise contrast between the conviction that the salvation of the nation is preordained—

Therefore say to the household of Israel, "Thus says the Lord God: It is not for your sake that I am about to act, O house of Israel, but for my holy name which you have caused to be profaned among the nations to which you came." (36:22) —

and the message of forgiveness which has its clearest expression until the time of Jesus in thse words of Ezekiel:

Therefore, O mortal man, say to the household of Israel: "Because you say, 'Our transgressions and our sins lie upon us, and under them we waste away; how then can we live?' as I live," is the oracle of the Lord God, "I have no pleasure in the death of the wicked, but rather in this, that the wicked man turn from his way and live. Turn, O turn, from your evil ways! Why should you die, O house of Israel?" (33:10-11.)

There are times when Ezekiel seems to say that the change of the individual will be due to the power of the Deity and not the choice of the individual. Even the changed heart is a result of the arbitrary plan of God and not to the changed allegiance of the worshiper. At other times the message is clear that true repentance of the individual is essential and with repentance there will be foregiveness from God:

"Therefore, O house of Israel, I will judge you each in accordance with his ways," is the oracle of the Lord God. "Repent, then, and turn from all your transgressions, lest your iniquity bring you to ruin. Cast away from you all the transgressions which you have committed against me; and get yourselves a new heart and a new spirit. Why should you die, O house of Israel? For I have no pleasure in the death of anyone who dies," is the oracle of the Lord God. "Turn, then, and live!" (18:30-32.)

His favorite description of man was "son of man," which was an expression that emphasized the utter weakness of humanity. He used it in contrast to the power which he ascribed to God. The contrast is vivid and purposely so. Nevertheless his standard for man was very high. Religion for Ezekiel was personal moral responsibility before God. Each man must stand trial for his conduct and for his alone. Ezekiel was in complete agreement with Jeremiah at this point, though it should be noted that it is doubtful if Ezekiel's followers had ever heard the message of Jeremiah, for Jeremiah was of no great importance until after the first deportation of prisoners. The Babylonian civilization into which the captives were taken was a very old one. It had developed many elaborate patterns of conduct, and none was more complex than that of Babylonian business. The Babylonian business world was a complicated structure, and records have been preserved which bear testimony to its elaborate organization. It was a system of private enterprise and private property. The Jews soon entered this new world of activity and were spectacularly successful. They discovered that the individual had a new significance in such an economy, and personal moral responsibility was of increased importance, such as they had not known formerly. Ezekiel went even further than Jeremiah in his insistence upon this principle of personal moral responsibility. He stated clearly that one individual could not be substituted for another. There was no transfer of merit or credit.

"O mortal man, if a land sin against me by acting teacherously, and I stretch out my hand against it, and break its staff of bread, and send famine upon it, and cut off from it man and beast, even though these three men were in the midst of it—Noah, Daniel, and Job—they would by their righteousness save but themselves," is the oracle of the Lord God. (14:13-14.)

Not only was each man personally responsible for his own moral conduct, but the standard was very high.

"If a man be righteous, and do what is lawful and right—if he eat no flesh with the blood in it, nor lift up his eyes to the idols of the house of Israel; if he defile not his neighbor's wife, nor approach a woman in the time of her uncleanness; if he oppress no one, but conscientiously restore the debtor's pledge; if he commit no robbery, but share his bread with the hungry, and cover the naked with a garment; if he lend no money at interest, nor take increase for himself; if he withhold his hand from crime, observe strict justice between man and man, follow my statutes, and be careful to observe my ordinances—he is righteous, and shall surely live," is the oracle of the Lord God. (18:5-9.)

That standard included the ceremonial demands of purity, the moral demands of purity, right conduct toward God and his laws, and right conduct toward one's fellow man. Ezekiel was not content with meeting only the obligations of ceremonial law. He set the pattern of man's conduct on an exceedingly high level.

The great ideal of Ezekiel was to have a part in the building of God's kingdom. The ideal kingdom would have God as its ruler, and peace would be there. But Ezekiel was not concerned with material prosperity and bounteous harvests that necessitated the enlarging of barns. He was concerned that God should reign in the hearts of men—hearts which have been made pliable and receptive to the law of God. Though there were strange behavior patterns of Ezekiel that are difficult of interpretation, yet his ideal for man and for the kingdom of God were the highest to be discovered in the Old Testament. The way to the kingdom was through sincere repentance, and here again it is significant that his message of repentance and forgiveness was closer to the message of Jesus than was that of any other prophet. Ezekiel was a prophet of God's kingdom.

16

A Continuing Journey

AS ONE TRAVELS SOUTHWEST FROM CASPER, WYOMING, TOWARD the Sweetwater River crossing, the traveler is close to the old trails of the pioneers. The road is long, and the journey is a weary one even with modern transportation. Suddenly there appears in the distance a rounded outline that is in strange contrast with the surrounding terrain. The traveler hastens on to discover a huge mound of solid rock. It is Independence Rock, known to the early pioneers as the "Register of the Desert." Upon it are inscribed the names of many travelers, pioneers as well as modern tourists. To read those names is to recall much of the history of the West, but not all who started with the wagon caravans reached that rock. Their names are not there. Many contributed to the opening of the West, the breaking of new trails, and the settling of the Rocky Mountain territory and the great Northwest. Only a few of their names may be read on Independence Rock, but the contributions of the unknown are none the less real. Not all who contributed to the development of Hebrew thought have their names inscribed in the Bible. Some are there, particularly those individuals whose positions of leadership and whose messages have inscribed their names large upon the pages of religious history. In later days the writer of Hebrews could speak of "such a crowd of witnesses" and included far more than I have been able to discuss in these pages. To all of them we are indebted, known or unknown heroes; for unless they had broken the trail and then painstakingly enlarged the trail to a broad highway, we should be faced with that task. There are still trails for man to break, but many great highways of religion have been built. Clergy and laity, prophet and priest, the Hebrews and his neighbor, have all contributed their portion; and the world has been enriched. As we have attempted to get better acquainted with these individuals and their messages, there are certain convictions that crowd in upon us.

Many and varied are the personalities of the men whose lives and teachings we have examined, yet an outstanding characteristic which each shares in common is that of complete consecration to his God. Some were not too much concerned with their fellow men, but they did have an urgency with which they devoted themselves to the task to which they felt themselves called. It led most of the prophets to an impatience that prevented them from seeing anything good other than in their own particular point of view. The balancing patience of the priest was urgently needed in order that the stirring words of the prophets might be preserved and built into the program of religious education and the accepted law of the community. Nevertheless the utter consecration of the prophets made them hold with tenacity to those things they believed of utmost significance, and the people were finally persuaded that these things were important. The prophet held nothing in reserve, and he used everything that was near and dear to him as a means of calling attention to his message. In most cases the message was rejected during the lifetime of the messenger, but he was vindicated by later generations. Only complete consecration could have sustained them in their hours of defeat.

The hopes and aspirations of the people have likewise played an important part in the development of religious thought. Religion is of the people, not confined to the institution or to the leaders. Theologians must build their systems of religion from the experiences that are common to all men. Similarly, as the ancient leaders gave consideration to the great problems with which men were confronted, they necessarily had to start at the point of their own and others' religious experiences. Just as the psychologist arrives at an understanding of patterns of behavior by testing the reactions of hundreds of subjects, just so the religious leader must arrive at any valid system of thought by examining religion in the lives of men. The prophets, consciously or unconsciously, arrived at their convictions because of their own religious experiences and the religious experiences of their fellow men. Yet at times they denied the hopes and aspirations of their fellows. Men hoped that there might be a hereafter, but none of the prophets gave encouragement to these hopes until shortly before the time of Jesus. The belief in a life hereafter was only a hope in Old Testament days. Men dreamed of an ideal world in which there would be satisfaction and peace. Their dreams became crassly materialistic at times, and at others there was complete pessimism toward man's ability to build an ideal community. Under the guidance of the prophets and the teachings of Jesus man has been encouraged in his hopes and expectations, and the Kingdom can come as man brings his life into harmony with the teachings of Christ and makes God the supreme power in his life. Still there are those who would retreat in despair and who fail to discover the potential of the divine spark within man. For them there is hope only in a kingdom which shall be imposed upon man in spite of the fact that the best traditions of our religion lead us to believe in a God who leads rather than drives men to loftier heights of living.

As we read the messages of the prophets of Judah and of Israel, we discover again and again that these men had a profound belief that God is the Lord of history; and as one reads, he suddenly discovers that he is coming with satisfaction to that same point of view. In the life and teachings of Jesus there is a focal point in history, and a historical examination of the records of the Old Testament indicates a progressive development that finds its culmination in Jesus. The pattern is not complete without him. The teachings of the prophets and the teachings and the death of Jesus fit together to betoken the love and concern that God has for us. One of the functions of religion is to bring peace where there has been frustration. A conviction that God is the Lord of history has given man a sense of destiny and of worth that was not possible from any other viewpoint. Coupled with that is the constant reiteration by the prophets and Jesus that God is "keeping watch above his own" and meets man in his need. When man failed to respond to one opportunity, another was provided. In one of his parables, the parable of the wicked husbandman (Matt. 21:33-42), Jesus illustrates this principle by telling of a succession of representatives who came and were rejected, until finally the owner of the vineyard sent his own son. It is a daring picture of God adjusting his program because man has been given freedom of choice.

We have examined in turn a succession of ideas and a succession of religious leaders. Whether we arrange the written documents or our knowledge of the teachers into chronological sequence, it becomes apparent that over the long sweep of history there has been progression of thought. One generation may slip back and another take great strides forward, but over the span of the years advance has been made. As men come to grips with problems, they can be benefited by all that has been proposed by those who preceded them. One of the confirmed habits of religion is to conserve the traditions of the past, particularly the good values it has discovered. This has made it possible for men in the religious tradition to build upon the great gains of the past and to come to ever-increasing heights of discovery. No leaders of thought are isolated fragments of humanity; they stand in a long line of succession. They may not recognize their indebtedness to their predecessors, but they have a debt nonetheless. The succession of ideas is apparent in the documents and in the lives of the men who produced them. Much of the literature must remain, at least for the present, without benefit of the author's identity. We have more literature than we have information concerning the writers. Yet the personality of the writers crowds in upon our consciousness again and again, and we are aware that religion cannot be a set of principles inscribed in a document but is the power and principle by which men live. Jesus said, "Follow Me." Religion is conviction at work in the life of a man.

The religious leaders in the Old Testament were a motley group of all sorts and conditions of men. Their personality traits were decidedly varied. No one type may be said to predominate. Each played his part, and each had his particular contribution to hand on to succeeding generations. Religious conviction is not confined to one psychological type, nor is an awareness of the divine presence restricted to one precise kind of individual. God is a respecter of human personality. These different individuals learned how to commune with God, and each became aware of his power and of his message to mankind.

These men did not agree in all respects concerning the nature of the Deity, and it is necessary to fit the messages of all of them into one comprehensive picture in order to get as complete an understanding as possible of the divine nature. But there was the same conviction with each one concerning the presence of God. Each was deeply aware that God was the companion of his life. Most outstanding of these men were the great prophets, for they bequeathed to posterity principles upon which could be built the message of Jesus of Nazareth. Their messages were not merely their conscientious reactions to the faults of their day nor insights that led to the solution of the problems involved, but out of their wrestling in the presence of God came the ringing words "Thus saith the Lord." They were men coming to grips with problems that had plagued mankind for many centuries, and they found through their religious experiences the answers that other men had failed to find. That is why our Bible is a book that throbs with life. It is alive with the heartthrobs of men and women who in the consciousness of the presence of God struggled with great human problems that surrounded them and their fellows. Out of the depths of human suffering and from the heights of human aspiration have come the great convictions that stem from vital religious living.

Index to Biblical References

Index to Persons and Subjects

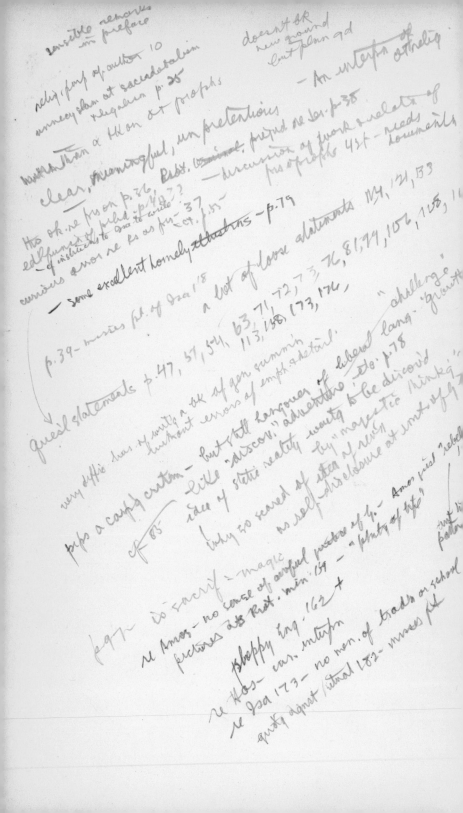